THE INTERNATIONAL COURT OF JUSTICE

Its Role in the Maintenance of International Peace and Security

United Nations Studies: No. 6

Carnegie Endowment for International Peace
United Nations Studies
ISBN 0-313-20320-2 UNSS

1. The Budget of the United Nations, 1947, *ISBN 0-313-20328-8 BUNN*

2. Coordination of Economic and Social Activities, 1948, *ISBN 0-313-20329-6 CESA*

3. Consultation Between the United Nations and Non-Governmental Organizations, 1949, *ISBN 0-313-20330-X COUN*

4. The United Nations Secretariat, 1950, *ISBN 0-313-20331-8 UNNS UNNS*

5. Voting and the Handling of Disputes in the Security Council, 1950, *by Eduardo Jiménez de Aréchaga, ISBN 0-313-20332-6 ARVH*

6. The International Court of Justice: Its Role in the Maintenance of International Peace and Security, 1951, *by Oliver James Lissitzyn, ISBN 0-313-20333-4 LICJ*

7. The Political Role of the General Assembly, 1951, *by Henry Field Haviland, ISBN 0-313-20334-2 HAPG*

8. Latin America in the United Nations, 1956, *by John A. Houston, ISBN 0-313-20335-0 HOLU*

9. The General Assembly of the United Nations, A Study of Procedure and Practice, 1964, *by Sydney Dawson Bailey, ISBN 0-313-20336-9 BAGA*

10. Field Administration in the United Nations System: The Conduct of International Economic and Social Programs, 1961, *by Walter Rice Sharp, ISBN 0-313-20337-7 SHFA*

11. The Secretariat of the United Nations, 1964, *by Sydney Dawson Bailey, ISBN 0-313-20338-5 BASU*

THE INTERNATIONAL COURT OF JUSTICE

Its Role in the Maintenance of International Peace and Security

By

OLIVER J. LISSITZYN
Department of Public Law and Government
Columbia University

United Nations Studies: No. 6

GREENWOOD PRESS, PUBLISHERS
WESTPORT, CONNECTICUT

Library of Congress Cataloging in Publication Data

Lissitzyn, Oliver James, 1912-
The International Court of Justice, its role in the maintenance of international peace and security.

Reprint of the 1951 ed. published by the Carnegie Endowment for International Peace, New York, which was issued as no. 6 of United Nations studies.
Bibliography: p.
1. Hague. International Court of Justice.
I. Title. II. Series: United Nations studies ; no. 6.
[JX1971.6.L5 1978] 341.5'5 78-2885
ISBN 0-313-20333-4

Reprinted in 1978 by Greenwood Press, Inc.
51 Riverside Avenue, Westport, CT. 06880

Printed in the United States of America

10 9 8 7 6 5 4 3 2 1

FOREWORD

I gladly comply with the invitation of the President of the Carnegie Endowment for International Peace to contribute a Foreword to this scholarly and timely monograph by Professor Lissitzyn on the International Court of Justice. For it is desirable that the work of the Court and its place in organised international society should be studied as a whole, and not only in relation to particular disputes or problems, however important. It is only then that we may hope to gain the proper perspective for assessing both the achievements of the Court and the scope of possible improvements in its constitutional structure and its methods. Such improvements are a legitimate subject of study and discussion notwithstanding the fact that as in the case of its predecessor — the Permanent Court of International Justice — the results of the first five years of the existence of the International Court of Justice have not only vindicated the expectations attached to its establishment at the end of the Second World War. They have exceeded it. In the first two years of the activity of the Court, the scarcity of cases submitted to it tended to create some embarrassment and prompted search for remote analogies of a similar predicament such as that of the Supreme Court of the United States which in the first decade after its establishment had a somewhat nominal existence. Yet, barely within five years of its creation, the number of cases inscribed on the list of the International Court of Justice suggests that the time may be near when the accumulation of business will render topical the question of the adaptation of the machinery of the Court to the rapid expansion of its contentious and advisory jurisdiction.

The actual and anticipated volume of the business of the Court is not the only indication or explanation of its present status and stature. There are rather reasons which seem to justify the statement that, probably, it has proved the most successful institution of the United Nations. One of the reasons for that achievement is the relative continuity of the composition of the Court, made possible by its Statute which provides for the retirement, every three years and subject to the possibility of re-election, of only one third of the membership of the Court. That continuity is calculated to secure not only a consistency and uniformity in the administration of the law, but also the creation of an articulate sense of collective and individual responsibility in the fifteen men who compose the "highest judicial organ" of the United Nations. That responsibility expresses itself in the by now firmly established tradition of solemnity and deliberation, bordering on formalism, in the conduct of the business of the Court; of studied restraint and punctilious discretion in the personal attitude of the judges; and, above all, in the fact that in many cases the Court has been in the position to make pronouncements on matters of importance by a vote which was unanimous or approaching unanimity. In most — practically all — international organs the representatives responsible for the conduct of their activities come and go; the continuity is that of the administrative personnel — an asset of inestimable value but necessarily of limited efficacy. In the Court the continuity is that of the principal organ as such. It is that factor — perhaps more than anything else — which has made it possible for the Court as a whole to live up to the tradition which was given powerful and memorable expression by President Huber on assuming office as President of the Court in 1925. He referred to the great responsibility of the Court — a responsibility which, he said, it might be too difficult to bear but for the consciousness that "so long as our [the Judges'] labours are devoted to the Cause . . . we are sustained by a force which is not merely our own."

It is in the light of the standing which the Court has thus acquired in the eyes of the world that there must be viewed the impact of its contribution to the maintenance of international peace. In the nature of things such contribution cannot be capable of direct proof. As within the State so also in the international sphere courts cannot properly assist the cause of peace by solving conflicts of political importance and by assuming functions which are essentially of a legislative nature. Neither is it the business of the Court to prevent actual outbreaks of violence. Nevertheless the peace preserving function of the Court may reveal itself in a variety of ways. In the first instance its very existence, even if not accompanied by compulsory jurisdiction, provides an opportunity for settling disputes on which both parties feel so strongly that having regard to domestic public opinion they would hesitate to adopt a solution by way of negotiations or compromise. Secondly, the existence of the Court, when endowed with compulsory jurisdiction, is a powerful factor in creating the atmosphere of respect for law. From that point of view the question as to the part of the Court in maintaining peace is almost tautologous. Peace cannot, in the long run, be preserved if law is flouted in reliance on the rule that members of the community are legally in the position to deny to others the opportunity of having disputed legal rights settled through an impartial determination by a judicial authority. For the same reason the effectiveness and the part of the Court as a factor in preserving peace must, ultimately, depend upon the scope of the jurisdiction which is conferred upon it. Such compulsory jurisdiction is not in itself a guarantee of peace or its only guarantee. But it is an important condition of peace which can be disregarded only at considerable peril and subject to a grave moral and political responsibility of States. From that point of view it must become axiomatic that at a time when nearly forty States have agreed to take the risks — for risks there are — and to assume the obligations of compulsory jurisdiction of the Court, there is no convincing justification for the remaining thirty States to withhold from it such jurisdiction. By the same token, at a time when ten States have accepted the compulsory jurisdiction of the Court without reservations there can be little justification for the others to qualify their acceptance by reservations. Explanations may be given for thus totally or partially withholding jurisdiction from the "highest judicial organ of the United Nations." Such explanations may be plausible. In the nature of things, they cannot be persuasive. In the same way as, in the words of the greatest President of the United States, the Union could not be at the same time half slave and half free, so also civilized States cannot in their mutual relations at the same time profess allegiance to law and deny it in its most vital aspect. There is a transparent incongruity in the spectacle of enlightened States invoking the supremacy of law and denying it by their actions. For that reason the problem of compulsory jurisdiction of the Court — voluntarily conferred upon it and subject to withdrawal — will, until solved in accordance with inescapable principle, continue to be the crucial problem of international judicial settlement and one of the crucial problems of international peace generally.

In the meantime, the absence of full compulsory jurisdiction need not prevent — and has not prevented — the International Court of Justice from continuing the work of its predecessor as an agency for clarifying and developing international law. The joint product of the work of the two Courts for a period of nearly a quarter of a century has been such as to cover most aspects of international law. The contribution of the Court in this sphere cannot be measured by the mere number of its Judgments and Advisory Opinions. This is so for the reason that one case may decide or throw illuminating light upon a multitude of points of interest for international law. Thus the Judgment in the *Corfu Channel* case is not only a contribution to the question of the position of international straits and the meaning of innocent passage. It is an authority, directly or indirectly, on other matters such as the right of intervention and self-help; interpretation of treaties, in particular of those conferring jurisdiction upon the Court; responsibility of States for injury done within their territory to other States; damages for breach of an international duty; and evidence in international proceedings. The brief Advisory Opinion on Reparation for Injuries Suffered in the Service of the United Nations provides authority not only on the question of the international personality of the United Nations. It also answers in a clear and emphatic manner the more general question of subjects of international law and of the standing of the Charter of the United Nations in relation to non-member States. Moreover, it is of importance for the question of the nationality of claims and for some significant aspects of interpretation of treaties. The same may be said of most Judgments and Advisory Opinions.

These wide possibilities, as revealed in the activity of the Court, of clarifying and developing international law raise the question of the technique and the contents, from that point of view, of its pronouncements. A judgment, even if it covers a variety of problems, may answer them in two ways: it may confine itself to a concise statement of the applicable rule or principle without any detailed elaboration of the reasons or precedents which have led to their adoption. The almost laconic *"considerants"* of the judgments of some French courts provide an example of that method. The elaboration is left to the commentators and authors of notes in the law reports. On the other hand, the decisions of the Court may follow the pattern of the detailed and elaborate judgments and opinions delivered by individual judges in England or in the United States and initiating the reader into the mental processes which have led to the decision, the juridical reasoning which underlies it, and the authorities — judicial and other — which support it or from which it must be distinguished. Great as is the standing of the Court, bare statements of the law can hardly have the same persuasive power as a pronouncement which by the force of its legal reasoning and its deliberate connection with previous practice and doctrine is calculated to become a contribution to international justice. It is possible that in so far as the Judgments and Advisory Opinions of the Court are the result not only of collective deliberation but also of collective drafting – it is difficult for the uninitiated to know whether this is in fact the method adopted – a somewhat drastic economy of expression may be the only feasible solution of the difficulty. But the question must remain whether that method is most conducive to the proper fulfilment of that particular function of the Court which consists not only in deciding a dispute or giving an opinion, but also in developing and clarifying international law.

There is, in addition, the further question whether collective drafting may not occasionally result in a tendency to compromise likely to interfere with the unity and, consequently, the usefulness and the authority of the judgment. Undoubtedly, some such compromise may be expressive of the inherent difficulties of the situation and may temper, in a manner consistent with justice and international progress, the rigidity of the existing law as interpreted by the Court. Of such possibilities the judgment of the Court, given in 1950, in the *Asylum Case* between Colombia and Peru provides an instructive example. On the one hand the Court held that it was "inconceivable" that the "urgent cases" which, according to the Havana Convention, alone justified the grant of asylum, should include "the danger of regular prosecution to which the citizens of any country lay themselves open by attacking the constitution of that country." This restrictive interpretation of the right to grant asylum may have been somewhat disturbing to those who see in political asylum an institution which has acquired a special and specific connotation in the relations of Latin American States. However, on the same page of the judgment the Court substantially mitigated the severity of the pronouncement as quoted. While reiterating the principle that asylum cannot be opposed to the operation of justice, it proceeded to qualify it by admitting an important exception in cases in which "in the guise of justice, arbitrary action is substituted for the rule of law" and in which administration of justice is "corrupted by measures prompted by political aims."

It must remain a matter for consideration whether the disadvantages inherent in a collective judgment and collective drafting — if collective drafting it be — are such as to call for a greater approximation to the Anglo-American method in which the judgment or opinion, even if given on behalf of the Court as a whole, are the product of an individual effort and, to that extent, of individual responsibility. As in other matters, there are also in this sphere tangible advantages in individual as distinguished from collective responsibility. Moreover, if — as is suggested in the concluding paragraphs of this Foreword — the accumulation of business may prove a relevant factor in the activity of the Court, it might become difficult for the Court as a whole to find the necessary time for assuming responsibility for every word and statement, as distinguished from their operative part, of its pronouncements. In the meantime, it is submitted that there is room for considering the best ways for making the Judgments and Opinions of the Court, under the present method of their preparation, as illuminating as possible. In addition, separate Opinions, fully consistent with the authority and dignity of the collective pronouncement, may fulfil an useful function in this connection.

Subject to these tentative and hesitating suggestions, it would be presumptuous for an outsider not acquainted with the intricacies of the deliberations of the Court to offer advice or to criticise the methods adopted. It is probable that the very continuity of the Court, which is one of its greatest assets and which enables it to profit by its own experience, will assist effectively in the solution of problems which as yet are of a baffling character. This applies, for instance, to the attitude of the Court to what is perhaps one of the most significant and controversial matters connected with its activity, namely, the use of so-called preparatory work in the interpretation of treaties. For while the interpretation of treaties is the most persistent and most significant part of the activity of the Court, the question of preparatory work is, in turn, probably the most important aspect of the function of interpretation. There are many – including scholars of weighty authority such as Professor Hyde – who believe that exclusive reliance on purely logical interpretation and the "plain" or "natural" meaning of words cannot provide an adequate guide for the essential function of interpretation – which is the discovery of the true intention of the parties. There are others who doubt, in particular in relation to multilateral treaties, whether there exists at all as ascertainable intention of the parties and whether recourse to complicated, bulky, often contradictory, and, in their view, unreliable "preparatory work" can be of assistance in the task of interpretation. The Permanent Court of International Justice, while laying down from time to time the general rule that there is no occasion to have recourse to preparatory work when the treaty is clear, did in fact resort to that instrument of interpretation. The International Court of Justice has acted more literally on the rule formally enunciated by its predecessor. Thus in the Advisory Opinion on the Competence of the General Assembly for the Admission of a State to the United Nations the Court stated that "if the relevant words in their natural and ordinary meaning make sense in their context, that it is the end of the matter." Having regard to these considerations the Court was of the opinion that "it is not permissible, in this case, to resort to *travaux préparatoires.*" It is possible that the ruling in this and similar cases may give rise to criticism. There is no occasion to deprecate such criticism as derogatory to the authority of the Court. They do not imply the suggestion that the Court may be inclined to circumvent, through the shortcut of a logical – and controversial – rule of interpretation, the laborious process of investigating in all requisite detail the cases submitted to it.

However, the problem thus raised by the question of "preparatory work" brings into prominence the issue, already referred to, of the time available to the Court for a full and meticulous enquiry into disputes and questions upon which it is called to decide or advise. The Court may be in the position to examine at leisure bulky preparatory work if the list of cases is so small that it can devote weeks — if not months — to the oral proceedings and the deliberations following upon them. It must be borne in mind that, in addition, a great deal of the time of the Court must be given to the study of the written pleadings in the cases pending before it. In the case of Judgments, these, as a rule, take the form of a Memorial, Counter-Memorial, Reply and Rejoinder — each of which may amount to a sizeable volume or volumes. Should, as must be hoped, the number of the cases submitted to the Court increase considerably — at the time of writing six cases are on the Court's list — the question will arise whether the necessary thorough investigation and deliberation does not call for a sub-division of the Court's work within the framework of its own organisation or possibly through some method of delegation or decentralization on a regional or some other basis. Thus, for instance, it might be a matter for consideration whether cases which are not of sufficient importance need be considered by the Court as a whole.

The same question will arise if and when the present rigid formulation of Article 34 of the Statute will be replaced by a more elastic provision. That Article, which lays down that States only can be parties to disputes before the Court, is based to a large extent on the orthodox view — which is increasingly ceasing to be orthodox — that States only can be subjects of international law. That view was unequivocally rejected by the unanimous Advisory Opinion of the Court in the case concerning the right of the United Nations to bring an international claim in respect of injuries suffered by its officials — an Opinion which will rank among the most significant pronouncements of the Court. In view of that Opinion, as well as other developments, there would appear to be no justification for preventing the Court from deciding, with the consent of States, disputes in which one of the parties is not a State.

It is the great merit of Professor Lissitzyn's book that, in a manner both stimulating and restrained, it calls for a discussion and study of these and similar questions well ahead of any formal examination by an international conference of the problem of the revision of the Statute of the Court. As such, in addition to its intrinsic merits, his book is timely in a very real sense and its publication under the auspices of the Carnegie Endowment for International Peace is a cause of satisfaction.

H. LAUTERPACHT.

June 1951.
Trinity College,
Cambridge.

TABLE OF CONTENTS

I. INTRODUCTION

The framers of the Charter of the United Nations, like those of the Covenant of the League of Nations, have provided for an agency whose principal function is to apply legal techniques in the resolution of international controversies and problems. This agency is the International Court of Justice, which is described in the Charter as one of "the principal organs" and as "the principal judicial organ" of the United Nations (Article 7 (1) and Article 92). With minor modifications, the organization and powers of the International Court of Justice are similar to those of the Permanent Court of International Justice in the League of Nations system, and its Statute, which forms an integral part of the Charter, is expressly based on the Statute of the old Court.[1]

The reputation of the Permanent Court of International Justice, unlike that of the League of Nations, had not been damaged by the failure of collective security in the interwar period. It had developed a tradition and a prestige by which the new Court was to benefit. However, since many of the enemy and neutral states continued to be parties to the old Statute, it was found technically easier to accomplish the necessary changes by the adoption of a new Statute and the creation of a new Court.

The members of the new Court were elected by the General Assembly and the Security Council in February 1946, and met for the first time in April. At the same time, the

[1] The Statute of the Permanent Court, however, was an instrument distinct from the Covenant of the League and membership in the League did not, as in the United Nations, *ipso facto* make a state a party to the Statute. Nevertheless, in both cases, it was provided that the expenses of the Court be borne by the international organization. In 1949 the Court's expenses amounted to $588,512. Of the total United Nations budget of $49,641,773 for 1950, the revised appropriation for the Court was $592,115. Provision is also made for contributions by parties to the Statute who are not members of the United Nations and by states which appear before the Court but are not parties to the Statute.

old Court was dissolved by a resolution of the Assembly of the League of Nations.

The purpose of this study is to appraise the Court as an instrument for the maintenance of international peace and security.[2] In what ways can it help to avoid resort to violence and war? What use has already been made of it? What unused potentialities does it have? The answers to these and other questions bearing on the role of the Court as an organ of the world community must be sought not only in the provisions of the Charter and the Statute, but also in the record of the Court, the attitude of the various states and of the political organs of the United Nations toward its functions, and the place of law in international relations.

The primary function of the United Nations is to maintain international peace and security. The means by which this function is to be carried out fall into three categories: (1) The creation and maintenance of conditions conducive to peaceful relations among states and to a general feeling of security; (2) peaceful settlement or adjustment of international disputes and situations likely to disturb friendly relations between states; (3) effective action to prevent or suppress breaches of the peace.

It is evident that these categories are interrelated. For example, success in the peaceful settlement of disputes and in the enforcement of peace may be expected to reduce fear and generate confidence, thereby helping to develop a feeling of genuine community among nations, which in turn may facilitate the further development of institutions for the maintenance of a prosperous, orderly and peaceful world. For purposes of analysis, however, it is convenient to think in terms of the three categories just stated.

---

[2] Since the International Court of Justice may be regarded for many purposes as a continuation of the Permanent Court of International Justice, the expression "the Court" (or "the International Court") is used in this study to describe the two Courts together as one continuing institution, unless otherwise indicated by the context. The abbreviations PCIJ and ICJ refer respectively to the old and the new Court.

II. THE COURT AND THE CONDITIONS OF INTERNATIONAL PEACE

Perhaps the greatest contribution that can be made by the Court to the cause of peace in the present stage of world organization is the development of international law through its activity. The proper appreciation of this contribution requires some understanding of the function of law as one of the conditions of peace among nations.

The Function of Law in the World Community

International lawyers recognize in principle that international law has grown and functioned largely in response to the practical needs of the world community, and students of international politics have accorded to international law a place, however modest, among the techniques of international relations; but no thorough study based on concrete historical data of the relation between international law and international politics has ever been made. The discussion here presented of the role of international law and its organs in the maintenance of peace and security is, therefore, of necessity general and in part based on certain reasonable but unproved hypotheses.[1]

---

1 For some discussions from various points of view of the nature of international law and its relation to world politics, see J. L. Brierly, *The Law of Nations* (4th ed., Oxford, The Clarendon Press, 1949) and *The Outlook for International Law* (Oxford, The Clarendon Press, 1944); Philip C. Jessup, "The Reality of International Law," *Foreign Affairs*, Vol. XVIII (1940), p. 244; Charles Cheney Hyde, *International Law Chiefly As Interpreted and Applied by the United States* (2nd revised ed., Boston, Little, Brown and Co., 1945), Vol. I, pp. 1-20; Edward Hallett Carr, *The Twenty Years' Crisis 1919-1939* (2nd ed., London, Macmillan Co., 1946), pp. 170-223; Hans J. Morgenthau, *Politics Among Nations* (New York, A. A. Knopf, 1948), pp. 209-42; Gerhart Niemeyer, *Law Without Force* (Princeton, Princeton University Press, 1941); Frederick Sherwood Dunn, *The Protection of Nationals* (Baltimore, The Johns Hopkins Press, 1932); Georg Schwarzenberger, "The Rule of Law and the Disintegration of the International Society," *American Journal of International Law,* Vol. 33 (1939), p. 56, and "International Law and Society," *The Year Book of World Affairs 1947,* p. 159; H. A. Smith, *The Crisis in the Law of Nations* (London, Stevens & Sons Ltd., 1947); Edwin D. Dickinson, "International Law: An Inventory,"

Peaceful coexistence of independent states (that is, states none of which is strong enough to impose its will on the others) in contact with each other is probably impossible without some commonly accepted standards of conduct. In the absence of such standards, states would not know what to expect of each other. They would not know where their authority ended and the authority of other states began. In the ordinary performance of governmental functions they would come into frequent collisions. Friction and temptation to resort to force would be very great.

Less directly, but perhaps even more effectively in the long run, the acceptance by states of some standards of conduct contributes to peace by fostering the growth of the interdependence of nations and international cooperation in the development of economic and social conditions conducive to stability. For example, international economic activity, such as trade and the development of resources with the assistance of foreign capital and technical experts, would be well-nigh impossible if the behavior of states toward foreigners within their reach were unpredictable. A stable relationship requires some standards defining and regulating it. The natural penalty for the disregard of such standards is the termination of the relationship.

The pattern of standards of conduct generally recognized by modern states as governing their mutual relations has come to be known as international law.[2] Basically it is customary law, developed by the slow and halting process of ostensibly voluntary modifications in the practices and attitudes of the various states. Sometimes a group of states wields enough influence to have its views crystallized into a generally accepted rule of international law; sometimes such a

California Law Review, Vol. 33 (1945), p. 506; Myres S. McDougal, "The Role of Law in World Politics," *Mississippi Law Journal,* Vol. 20 (1949), p. 253. On law in general, see Julius Stone, *The Province and Function of Law* (Sydney, Associated General Publications, 1946); Hans Kelsen, *General Theory of Law and State* (Cambridge, Harvard University Press, 1945).

2 Recently it has come to be recognized that international law also governs the relations of public international organizations with each other and with states.

rule results from a compromise of divergent interests. Its function, that of regulating the relations among the members and organs of the world community, is similiar to that of law in more highly organized communities. Lawyers and philosophers have at times questioned the propriety of calling this pattern "law," since unlike other civilized systems of law it has not generally been administered by judicial techniques nor enforced by superior authority. Nevertheless, no state today denies the existence or the legal character of international law, and in practice legal techniques and concepts have been found helpful in the discussion, interpretation and application of the standards of interstate conduct. The use of the term "law" to describe these standards is thus pragmatically justified.

Many of the standards of international law are observed as well as or even better than some of the standards of national law enforceable by superior authority. This has been true, for instance, of the hard core of the principles of diplomatic immunities and of the freedom of the seas in time of peace.

> Violations of law are rare in all customary systems, and they are so in international law. The explanation of that fact is simple, and so too is the explanation of the common belief to the contrary. For the law is normally observed because, as we shall see, the demands that it makes on states are generally not exacting, and on the whole states find it convenient to observe it; but this fact receives little notice because the interest of most people in international law is not in the ordinary routine of international legal business, but in the occasions, rare but generally sensational, on which it is flagrantly broken. Such breaches generally occur either when some great political issue has arisen between states, or in that part of the system which professes to regulate the conduct of war. But our diagnosis of what is wrong with the system will be mistaken if we fail to realize that the laws of peace and the great majority of treaties are on the whole regularly observed in the daily intercourse of states.[3]

In the absence of organized authority superior to the independent state, the principal sanctions of international law,

---

[3] J. L. Brierly, *The Law of Nations*, pp. 72-73.

aside from unilateral use of force the effectiveness of which depends on the power relationship between the contestants, are the disadvantages incurred by its breach, including the termination of the relations regulated by it and retaliation. Rational appreciation of the advantages of a relationship acts as a restraint upon the temptations to disregard the standards governing the relationship. For example, a state which persistently fails to respect the privileges and immunities of foreign diplomatic representatives may find itself excluded from diplomatic intercourse with the rest of the world. Furthermore, since the stronger nations have a preponderant influence in the development of some rules of international law, they often find it advantageous to support the observance of such rules. These sanctions are reinforced by the principles of moral obligation and good faith, the influence of public opinion, the advantages of a reputation for integrity and fair dealing, and the force of habit.

They may not always suffice to deter a strong state from working its will in disregard of international law. A state which attaches greater value to the attainment of certain objectives than to the preservation of peaceful relations will not be restrained by international law alone from resorting to force. Furthermore, the rational interest in the observance of law depends on a conviction that the existing order will endure. In times of great struggles for power, survival takes precedence over law. The existence of international law as we know it must, therefore, be regarded as probably a necessary, but not a sufficient, condition of peace. It makes peace possible but does not guarantee it.

The primary social function of any system of law is not merely to provide the rules for the settlement of disputes, but to prescribe and enforce standards of conduct deemed to be necessary or conducive to the preservation and advancement of the community. Among such standards are those designed to reduce friction between the members of the community and thereby prevent conflicts between them. Although in recent centuries there has been increasing emphasis on the development of standards and techniques designed to facilitate activities, such as travel, transportation, trade and investment, which cut across state boundaries, general international law — as distinguished from rules contained in treaties — is still largely composed of standards delimiting the jurisdiction of states and thus helping to avert clashes arising from conflicting claims of authority.[4]

The Need for the Development of International Law

The standards of international law vary in clarity, specificity and the extent of general acceptance, and the pattern as a whole is far from perfect. For example, the lack of universal recognition of a set of rules defining the limits of a state's territorial waters has continued to produce difficulties and disputes. Standards limiting the freedom of a state to determine what persons are its nationals, although recognized as existing in principle, are extremely vague and have not prevented the occurrence of dual nationality with resulting conflicts of allegiance and jurisdiction. The extent to which diplomatic immunities must be accorded to the subordinate personnel of a diplomatic mission is still a matter of disagreement. Rules for the termination of treaties are unsettled. Uncertainty as to the existence and content of standards limiting the freedom of states to deal as they please with the interests of foreign nationals within their territory has in recent years interfered with international economic activity and led to serious friction between some states. These are but a few examples of the inadequacies of the substantive content of international law.

It must not be thought, however, that the international community is incapable of working out standards that are generally accepted. The last forty years have seen the development of one of the most universally accepted and observed principles of international law — the principle that every state has sovereignty over the air space above its terri-

---

[4] See J. L. Brierly, *The Outlook for International Law*, p. 9.

tory. Many other rules and principles are just as firmly established. Nor must it be thought that any system of law can consist of absolutely clear and certain standards. Life, in its infinite variety and constant change, makes that impossible. In human relations, no two situations are exactly alike in their facts, and no one can predict with certainty the impact of changing conditions on the social significance of a particular situation. Legal standards, even when they are called "principles" or "rules," have fuzzy edges. There is always room for refinement and adjustment. In international law, however, the fuzziness of edges is probably greater than in most other systems of law. Therein lies a weakness of international law as an instrument for reducing international tensions.

The causes of this condition are deep-seated. Most of the historically recorded systems of law have been developed by a combination of three processes: (1) Habitual adherence of the members of the community to certain lines of conduct (custom); (2) Express enactment of standards of behavior binding on all the members of the community to whom the enactment applies regardless of their consent (statutory legislation); (3) Repetition and generalization of decisions made by the decision-making authorities (such as courts) with binding effect in particular controversies (precedent or case law). Since international law has developed in a community of independent states, there has been no single organ possessed of authority to resolve by express enactment or by adjudication with binding effect the clashes of policy and interest that frequently occur between groups of states. There is no world legislature. Treaty-making, although it is of great importance in supplementing the rules of general international law, is not an entirely adequate substitute for legislation, since treaties are binding only on states which agree to be bound by them, and very few treaties have had universal acceptance.[5]

---

[5] For further discussion of the problem of codification of international law, see pp. 68-71.

Judicial Decisions in the Development of International Law

Even when a standard appears to have gained general acceptance, or the acceptance of at least some of the states, its application to a particular set of facts may become a matter of dispute. In most systems of law, such disputes are usually referred to judicial tribunals for settlement; the decisions of such tribunals, whether or not they are regarded as legally binding precedents, serve to clarify the content and scope of the standards and become guides for future conduct. This is true even where the standards have been laid down in expressly enacted texts such as statutes or treaties. Legislative language is necessarily general, since no legislator can foresee all future contingencies. Furthermore, judicial decisions also help in the development of the law by exposing deficiencies in the existing standards and thereby making evident the need for remedial legislation.

Arbitral Tribunals

In the international community, there has never been universal acceptance of the authority of a judicial tribunal to give judgments with binding effect between states. Nevertheless, since the end of the eighteenth century, states have on numerous occasions submitted their disputes to arbitral tribunals for binding decisions. The judgments of international tribunals are not regarded as binding precedents for future cases, but a line of consistent decisions carries a great deal of weight. The many thousands of awards made by arbitral tribunals have helped to give more definite shape to international law standards, particularly in the field of responsibility of states for injuries to foreign nationals. These decisions have occupied a prominent place in many discussions of international law, on both official and unofficial levels. "The maximum of relative certainty is presented by the decisions of international Courts and tribunals."[6]

[6] Georg Schwarzenberger, *International Law,* Vol. I, *International Law as Applied by International Courts and Tribunals* (2nd ed., London, Stevens & Sons Ltd., 1949), p. li.

Arbitration has also helped to make the standards established by multilateral treaties more specific. Many such treaties contain provisions for their interpretation, in case of dispute, by arbitral bodies.

The influence exercised by the decisions of a particular international tribunal varies with such factors as the esteem in which its members are generally held, their impartiality, freedom from political motivation, thoroughness, the opportunities afforded to the parties for presenting and fully arguing their respective positions, and the cogency of the grounds given in support of the judgments.

Although the various arbitral tribunals have made a substantial contribution to the development and refinement of international law, their authority has been impaired by lack of continuity in functions, personnel and traditions, the narrowness of the basis of their powers (in most cases, agreements between the states immediately concerned), the differences in the personal characteristics and professional standing of the persons composing them, the suspicion that some arbitrators are unduly swayed by political considerations, and the failure of some tribunals to support their decisions by publishing reasoned opinions. The limited range of their influence is shown by the fact that it was still possible in 1895 for an eminent writer to declare that "there is no place for the refinements of the courts in the rough jurisprudence of nations."[7]

Creation of a Permanent Court

Until 1922 there was no standing international tribunal to which states in all parts of the world could submit their controversies for judicial settlement. The Permanent Court of Arbitration, set up under the Hague Conventions of 1899 and 1907 for the Pacific Settlement of International Disputes, was merely a panel of persons from which arbitrators to try particular cases between states could be selected by the states concerned.

---

[7] William Edward Hall, *A Treatise on International Law* (4th ed., Oxford, The Clarendon Press, 1895), p. 356 n. 2.

At the Second Peace Conference at The Hague in 1907, the process of arbitration was criticized as affording "no basis for the cumulation of a body of jurisprudence," and a draft convention was prepared, calling for the establishment of a standing Court of Arbitral Justice "of free and easy access, composed of judges representing the various judicial systems of the world, and capable of ensuring continuity in arbitral jurisprudence."[8] Although disagreement as to the number and method of appointment of the judges prevented action, the work of the Conference laid the foundation for a new and more fruitful effort to set up a true international court.

Article 14 of the Covenant directed the Council of the League of Nations to:

> formulate and submit to the Members of the League for adoption plans for the establishment of a Permanent Court of International Justice. The Court shall be competent to hear and determine any dispute of an international character which the parties thereto submit to it. The Court may also give an advisory opinion upon any dispute or question referred to it by the Council or by the Assembly.

The Statute of the Court thus envisaged was drafted in 1920 by a Committee of Jurists appointed by the Council, debated and modified by the Council and the Assembly of the League, and opened for adoption by states in December 1920.

The extent to which the bodies which took part in the drafting of the Statute were aware of the possibilities of the development of international law by the Court is not clear. The subcommittee of the Third Committee stated that one of the important tasks of the Court would be "to contribute through its jurisprudence, to the development of international law,"[9] and the British representative said that the

[8] Manley O. Hudson, *The Permanent Court of International Justice 1920-1942* (New York, Macmillan Co., 1943), pp. 80-81; H. Lauterpacht, *The Development of International Law by the Permanent Court of International Justice* (London, Longmans, Green and Co., 1934), pp. 2-3. The term "jurisprudence" here means case law.

[9] League of Nations, Records of the First Assembly, Meetings of the Committees, I, p. 534.

Court's decisions could not but "have the effect of gradually moulding and modifying international law," although he did not think "this was contemplated by the Covenant."[10] There is, however, no clear indication that this was representative of the general opinion and Article 59 of the Statute was worded as follows: "The decision of the Court has no binding force except between the parties and in respect to that particular case." This provision undoubtedly left the Court free not to regard a particular decision as a formally binding precedent for subsequent cases, but its intended impact on the role of the Court in the development of international law is not certain and has given rise to some controversy.[11]

Article 38 of the Statute directed the Court to apply, "as subsidiary means for the determination of rules of law" and "subject to the provisions of Article 59," "judicial decisions and the teachings of the most highly qualified publicists of the various nations." This provision has been generally understood to enable the Court to give considerable weight to its own previous decisions, although it is not formally bound by them, and the law-developing function of the Court has continued to be recognized in official utterances.

In 1929 the British government, in accepting the jurisdiction of the Court under the "optional clause" of the Statute, said that in comparison with codification "the method of building up a body of law by a series of legal decisions, a method which produced the English Common Law, may be the more suitable for at any rate some important branches of the Law of Nations."[12] In 1944 the Informal Inter-Allied Committee on the Future of the Permanent Court of International Justice said that what Article 59 "means is not that the decisions of the Court have no effect

---

[10] *Ibid.*, p. 512.

[11] Manley O. Hudson, *op. cit.*, pp. 195 and 207; H. Lauterpacht, *op. cit.*, pp. 4-5.

[12] Great Britain, Parliamentary Papers, Miscellaneous No. 12, *Memorandum on the Signature by His Majesty's Government in the United Kingdom of the Optional Clause of the Statute of the Permanent Court of International Justice,* Cmd. 3452 (1929), p. 8.

as precedents for the Court or for international law in general, but that they do not possess the binding force of particular decisions in the relations between the countries who are parties to the Statute. . . . [It] in no way prevents the Court from treating its own judgments as precedents, and indeed it follows from Article 38 . . . that the Court's decisions are themselves 'subsidiary means for the determination of rules of law.' "[13]

At the San Francisco Conference in 1945, Señor Perez of Venezuela, President of the Commission charged with the drafting of the Statute of the new Court, in his opening remarks at the first meeting of the Commission said: "Through its jurisprudence the Court will furthermore perform an essential function in giving the proper interpretation to the rules of international law."[14] Although Article 59 of the old Statute was reproduced *verbatim* in the Statute of the new Court, Secretary of State Stettinius, in his report to the President of the United States on the San Francisco Conference, declared:

> International law has long been criticized for its vagueness and its weakness. . . . The International Court of Justice, which the Charter establishes, has an important part to play in developing international law just as the courts of England and America have helped to form the common law.[15]

The International Court of Justice, like its predecessor, is undoubtedly a more effective instrument for the development of international law than an arbitral tribunal set up to dispose of a particular controversy. Its existence rests upon the agreement of most of the states of the world;[16]

---

[13] Great Britain Parliamentary Papers, Miscellaneous No. 2, *Report of the Informal Inter-Allied Committee on the Future of the Permanent Court of International Justice, 10th February, 1944,* Cmd. 6531 (1944), p. 19.

[14] *The United Nations Conference on International Organization, Selected Documents* (Washington, Government Printing Office, 1946), p. 883.

[15] *Charter of the United Nations: Report to the President on the Results of the San Francisco Conference by the Chairman of the United States Delegation, The Secretary of State,* Department of State Publication 2349 (26 June 1945), p. 138.

[16] As of 1 February 1951, the parties to the Statute include all the Members of the United Nations, Switzerland and Liechtenstein. Between 1921 and

its membership is stable and widely representative of the major geographical regions and legal systems of the world, and is not, for the most part, determined by the parties to a particular dispute; its standards and traditions rest upon the cumulative integrity, wisdom and experience of the many eminent international jurists who have sat on its predecessors' and its own Bench, and may be expected to follow an unbroken line of development; its location at The Hague permits a measure of detachment from the political atmosphere of the seat of the United Nations; the continuity of its organization, functions and personnel makes for consistency in its approach to legal problems and the nature of its tasks; the great library at its disposal and the staff of the Registry provide better aids to study and research than those available to most arbitrators; the freedom of its members, who receive an annual salary and are expected to devote full time to their duties, permits concentration on their judicial work; its rules provide for full presentation in written pleadings and oral arguments of the positions of the interested states and of public international organs;[17] and it is required to state the reasons for its decisions and to permit any member to deliver a separate concurring or dissenting opinion.

The Court's function in the development of international law can be exercised not only in connection with the adjudication of contentious cases, but also in connection with the rendering of advisory opinions. Under Article 96 of the Charter –

> 1. The General Assembly or the Security Council may request the International Court of Justice to give an advisory opinion on any legal question.
>
> 2. Other organs of the United Nations and specialized agencies, which may at any time be so authorized by the General

1942 fifty-one states became parties to the Statute of the Permanent Court but neither the United States nor the Soviet Union was among them.

[17] In a complicated case the pleadings and the transcript of the arguments may be thousands of pages long.

Assembly, may also request advisory opinions of the Court on legal questions arising within the scope of their activities.[18]

The Statute, in Article 68, provides that in "the exercise of its advisory functions the Court shall further be guided by the provisions of the present Statute which apply in contentious cases to the extent to which it recognizes them to be applicable." The task of giving advisory opinions has been uniformly treated by the Court as a judicial one. In fact, the Rules and practices of the Court have assimilated the procedure leading to advisory opinions as much as possible to that followed in contentious cases. Liberal provision is made for allowing interested states and international organizations to make written and oral statements and to comment on each other's positions in advisory proceedings.

Nevertheless, some unavoidable differences remain. When an advisory proceeding relates to a legal question actually pending between two or more states, the statements made by the interested states may be normally expected to amount to a substantial equivalent of the pleadings and arguments in contentious cases; when, however, an advisory opinion is requested on a question not directly related to an actual dispute, states and international organizations may fail, for various reasons, to develop before the Court all the possible considerations bearing on the question, and the presentation may be consequently one-sided. This actually happened in the proceedings leading to the advisory opinion on the capacity of the United Nations to claim reparation for injuries suffered in the service of the United Nations,[19] when no state or international organization squarely challenged before the Court the existence of such capacity,[20] although in the discussions of the question in the Sixth Committee of

---

18 See further, Articles 65-68 of the Statute. Under Article 14 of the Covenant of the League of Nations, the Council and the Assembly could request an advisory opinion on "any dispute or question." No other organ had such power.

19 ICJ Reports 1949, p. 174.

20 *Reparation for Injuries Suffered in the Service of the United Nations*, ICJ Pleadings 1949, *passim*.

the third session of the General Assembly, the capacity had been denied by at least one delegate;[21] nevertheless, as will be seen below, the weight of the Court's opinion does not seem to have been in practice unfavorably affected thereby, probably because the answers of the Court to the questions put before it were felt to be responsive to the needs of the international community.

A potentially serious deficiency of advisory opinions as an instrument for the development of international law lies also in their lack of formal binding force. Should the requesting international organ, or an interested state, choose to exercise its formal right to disregard the opinion and proceed to act in a manner inconsistent with it, the authority of the opinion as a statement of existing law would be clouded. Repeated instances of such behavior could not but undermine the influence of the Court and throw doubt on the value of its pronouncements as guides for the future conduct of states and international organs.

Limitations of Judicial Tribunals

The role of any judicial tribunal in the development of law must of necessity be a limited one. Much of the law-developing function is performed indirectly when the results of the proceedings before it make manifest the inadequacies of the existing legal standards which it is powerless to disregard. No court is expected, normally, to cut new law out of whole cloth. It has to work within the existing legal, political and social framework. Too radical a departure from the accepted standards and attitudes exposes a court to the charge of usurpation of power and may put an end to its usefulness. This is especially true of an international tribunal such as the International Court of Justice, whose powers rest entirely upon the voluntary submission of the various states and whose decisions are not regularly enforced

21 See the views of Spiropoulos, the Greek delegate, General Assembly, Official Records: Third Session, Part I, Sixth Committee, Summary Records of Meetings, 21 September-10 December 1948, pp. 530-32.

by the organized strength of the community. The Court must proceed with caution if it is not to lose the confidence of governments and, consequently, its powers and authority. An innovation not generally acceptable to states will not be followed by them in practice and will thus fail to make a real contribution to the development of international law.

Furthermore, the Court's law-developing function cannot be exercised apart from the cases brought to it. The immediate function of a judicial tribunal is to decide a concrete controversy or to give an opinion on a specific question. The proper exercise of this function requires the tribunal to examine and pass upon the contentions advanced by the various parties and such further considerations as the tribunal finds to be directly relevant to the issues before it. A judicial tribunal is not expected to produce academic essays upon questions merely suggested by the cases but not necessary for their decision, particularly if the parties do not have the opportunities or do not deem it necessary to argue such questions fully before it. An academic essay produced by a judicial tribunal, though perhaps entitled to respect as representing the views of some eminent jurists, does not have the authority of the reasoning necessary to support a judgment or advisory opinion.

The influence and usefulness of a decision is enhanced, on the other hand, by a full presentation and discussion of the reasoning behind it. Its usefulness as a guide for the future may also be enhanced by separate opinions, whether concurring or dissenting, which, as the experience of such tribunals as the Supreme Court of the United States indicates, may provide valuable help for understanding the true import of the decision and its alternatives. Furthermore, the law-developing function of a tribunal is dependent to a considerable degree on the attitude of the parties appearing before it, since it is up to the parties, in the first instance, to frame and develop the issues before the court. This, again, is particularly true of international tribunals whose jurisdiction rests on the consent of the parties and which, therefore, have little power to determine the scope of the issues they have to decide.

Even when all the circumstances are favorable, development of the law by judicial decisions is a slow, unspectacular and never-ending task, the accomplishment of which can only be estimated in rough and comparative terms. The courts of England have been developing the common law for more than seven centuries — can it be said that the task is finished? The development of the law ends only when the history of the community in which it takes place comes to an end. So long as the community lives, it cannot remain static; new conditions, new needs, call for new standards and interpretations.

The Court's Contribution to International Law

It is evident that the contribution of the two Courts to the development of international law in the brief twenty-nine years of their existence — including seven years of standstill resulting from the second World War — cannot have been very great in absolute terms, and that its magnitude cannot be accurately measured or stated. No scientific technique has yet been found to measure the growth of the law. Nor can any definite statement be ventured as to the extent to which the development of international law by the Court has so far contributed to the maintenance of international peace and security. Some tentative observations, however, may be made with respect to the attitude with which the Court has approached its law-developing function, the highlights and results of its law-developing activity, and the conditions affecting the magnitude and value of its contribution to international law.

Use of Precedents

Article 59 of the Statute, as already explained, enables the Court to regard itself as not formally bound by its own precedents. In fact, however, the Court refers constantly to its own previous decisions and pronouncements, and has never admitted that any two of its judgments or opinions have been inconsistent. It has expressly referred to a previous advisory opinion as a "precedent."[22] When there is danger that the Court will be accused of inconsistency, it takes pains to "distinguish" its previous action in a manner very reminiscent of the traditional technique of getting around precedents used by the Anglo-American common law courts and lawyers.

A striking recent example of this technique appears in the advisory opinion of 30 March 1950, on the interpretation of peace treaties with Bulgaria, Hungary and Rumania, in which the Court rejected the argument that it should not give the requested opinion because Bulgaria, Hungary and Rumania were not members of the United Nations or parties to the Statute of the Court and had not given their consent to a judicial proceeding relating to a legal question pending between them and other states. Referring to the Eastern Carelia case, in which the Court had declined in 1923 to give an opinion at the request of the Council of the League of Nations on the nature, interpretation and effect of certain instruments to which Soviet Russia was a party, after the Soviet government had objected to the proceeding, the Court said:

> In the opinion of the Court, the circumstances of the present case are profoundly different from those which were before the Permanent Court of International Justice in the Eastern Carelia case (Advisory Opinion No. 5), when that Court declined to give an Opinion because it found that the question put to it was directly related to the main point of a dispute actually pending between two States, so that answering the question would be substantially equivalent to deciding the dispute between the parties, and that at the same time it raised a question of fact which could not be elucidated without hearing both parties. As has been observed, the present Request for an

[22] Interpretation of the Greco-Turkish Agreement of 1 December 1926, PCIJ, *Publications*, Series B, No. 16, p. 15. See further, H. Lauterpacht, *op. cit.*, pp. 4 ff., and Manley O. Hudson, *op. cit.*, pp. 626-30.

Opinion is solely concerned with the applicability to certain disputes of the procedure for settlement instituted by the Peace Treaties, and it is justifiable to conclude that it in no way touches the merits of those disputes. . . . It follows that the legal position of the parties to these disputes cannot be in any way compromised by the answers that the Court may give to the Questions put to it.[23]

It is not necessary to pass judgment here on the merits of the distinction made by the Court in this case. Suffice it to note that the Court avoided overruling a precedent, even though it was technically a new Court, distinct from the Permanent Court of International Justice.[24] The attitude of the Court toward precedents is thus strikingly reminiscent of the attitude of the Anglo-American courts. In Anglo-American law, it is true, there is a doctrine, often referred to as the doctrine of *stare decisis,* of the binding force of precedents. This doctrine is still widely respected, at least in theory, but the Supreme Court of the United States has on numerous occasions overruled its own precedents.[25] Article 59 of the Statute cannot serve, therefore, as the basis for any far-reaching conclusions as to the difference between the role of precedent in the development of international law by the

---

[23] ICJ Reports 1950, p. 72. The three dissenting judges disagreed with this distinction and extensively cited and analyzed the Eastern Carelia case as a precedent supporting their dissent. *Ibid.,* pp. 90-92, 102-04, 108-11. See also the separate opinion of Judge Azevedo, *ibid.,* pp. 81-82, 85-86, 87-88. For some earlier examples of distinctions made by the Court to prevent the charge of inconsistency, see H. Lauterpacht, *op. cit.,* pp. 6-7, and advisory opinion on Interpretation of the 1919 Convention Concerning Employment of Women During the Night, PCIJ, *Publications,* Series A/B, No. 50, p. 378.

[24] The new Court has in several cases indicated reliance on precedents in the decisions of the Old Court. See, *e.g.,* Corfu Channel Case (Preliminary Objection), ICJ Reports 1948, p. 28; Admission of a State to the United Nations (Charter, Art. 4), Advisory Opinion, ICJ Reports 1948, p. 63; Competence of Assembly Regarding Admission to the United Nations, Advisory Opinion, ICJ Reports 1950, p. 8.

[25] For a provocative recent discussion of the place of *stare decisis* in American law, see the address delivered by Mr. Justice William O. Douglas before the Association of the Bar of the City of New York on 12 April 1949, printed under the title "Stare Decisis" in *Columbia Law Review,* Vol. 49 (1949), p. 735. Although in the continental legal systems, the doctrine of *stare decisis* does not exist, precedent has come to play an increasingly important role in the development of law. The Statute and practice of the Court largely reflect continental doctrine and practice.

International Court and its modern role in the development of Anglo-American law.

The reasons for the similarities in the use of precedent are not hard to find:

> The Court follows its own decisions for the same reasons for which all courts – whether bound by the doctrine of precedent or not – do it, namely, because such decisions are a depository of legal experience to which it is convenient to adhere; because they embody what the Court thinks is the law; because respect for decisions given in the past makes for continuity and stability, which are of the essence of orderly administration of justice; and because judges do not like, if they can help it, to admit that they were previously in the wrong.[26]

Developing the Law

Does the Court's policy of respect for its own precedents imply an unprogressive attitude? Is the Court likely to cling to an obsolete standard merely because it is already embedded in its own previous pronouncements? The danger of undue conservatism and stagnation is always present in the law. If precedent is taken too seriously, it becomes an obstacle to progress. Even very conservative courts, however, contribute to the development of law when their decisions make the need for changes clear.[27] The history of the Court is too short to permit a definitive judgment on the long-range significance of its respect for precedent. There is no indication, however, that respect for its own precedents has ever prevented the Court from making a decision that it considered right. It is also clear that the Court is fully alive to the evolving nature of international law, and that it will not

---

26 H. Lauterpacht, *op. cit.*, p. 8. "Any tribunal which seeks to administer justice in an impersonal manner will be disposed to rely on precedents where they exist." Manley O. Hudson, *op. cit.*, p. 627.

27 Some writers attach considerable importance to the work of the Court as laying the ground for the necessary reforms in international law. See, *e.g.*, A. Hammarskjöld, *Juridiction Internationale* (Leiden, A. W. Sijthoff, 1938), p. 249. On the efforts to change by treaty the law applied by the Court in the *Lotus* case, see Philip C. Jessup, "The Growth of the Law," *American Journal of International Law*, Vol. 29 (1935), p. 495.

be held back from serving the needs of the international community by lack of precedent either in its own decisions or elsewhere. In the Fourth Advisory Opinion, given in 1923, the Court said:

The question whether a certain matter is or is not solely within the jurisdiction of a State is an essentially relative question; it depends upon the development of international relations. Thus, in the present state of international law, questions of nationality are, in the opinion of the Court, in principle within the reserved domain.[28]

A striking example of the feeling of the Court that the development of international law must keep abreast of the needs of the international community is afforded by its advisory opinion on the capacity of the United Nations to claim reparation for injuries suffered in the service of the United Nations. The Court, as it recognized, was faced here with a new situation. Lack of precedent did not deter it, however, from unanimously holding that the United Nations is an international person which has the capacity in international law to bring claims against states, including nonmembers. The general approach of the Court to the problem is shown in the following passage:

The subjects of law in any legal system are not necessarily identical in their nature or in the extent of their rights, and their nature depends upon the needs of the community. Throughout its history, the development of international law has been influenced by the requirements of international life, and the progressive increase in the collective activities of States has already given rise to instances of action upon the international plane by certain entities which are not States. This development culminated in the establishment in June 1945 of an international organization whose purpose and principles are specified in the Charter of the United Nations. But to achieve these ends the attribution of international personality is indispensable.[29]

---

[28] Nationality Decrees Issued in Tunis and Morocco (French Zone) on 8 November 1921, PCIJ, *Publications,* Series B, No. 4, p. 24.

[29] ICJ Reports, pp. 178 and 182.

The Court then resorted to the doctrine of implied powers, finding support for it, on the international plane, in the Thirteenth Advisory Opinion of the Permanent Court of International Justice given in 1926 with respect to the powers of the International Labour Organisation.[30]

Worthy of special mention in this connection is also the advisory opinion on the international status of South West Africa, in which the Court held that the United Nations, in place of the League of Nations, was entitled to supervise the administration of a Mandate.[31]

The Court, like most other judicial tribunals, must try to balance the need for stability and certainty of the law on one hand, and the need for its progressive development on the other. Like most courts, it is loath to avow its law-making function in so many words, but already in 1934 it was possible for a distinguished commentator to say that "debarred from directly acting as a supreme agency for peace, the Court has consciously and, with few exceptions, consistently fulfilled its secondary function, namely, the developing of international law."[32]

How much has it actually contributed to international law? There are many fields of the law which have remained virtually untouched by the Court, and it would be impossible to present a complete picture of the modern law of nations relying upon the pronouncements of the Court alone. As already stated, its contribution to international law, owing to the shortness of its existence, cannot have been very great in absolute terms. In the eighteen years of its judicial activity, the Permanent Court of International Justice rendered twenty-one judgments on the merits of contentious cases (including questions of the amount of compensation due), two judgments interpreting previous judgments, and nine judgments dealing with preliminary questions (including questions of the jurisdiction of the Court and intervention of interested states in the proceedings); it also responded to

30 PCIJ, *Publications,* Series B, No. 13. This is another instance of the new Court relying on a precedent set by PCIJ.

31 ICJ Reports 1950, p. 128.

32 H. Lauterpacht, *op. cit.,* p. 2.

twenty-seven requests for advisory opinions.[33] In the four years of the judicial activity of the new Court (1947-1950), it has given four judgments on the merits of contentious cases (including a request for interpretation of a judgment), and one judgment on a preliminary objection; it has also delivered six advisory opinions.

Years	*Cases Submitted*	*Cases Withdrawn*	*Judgments*	*Advisory Opinions*
1922-1940	61	11	32	27
1941-1946	0	0	0	0
1947	2	0	0	0
1948	1	0	1	1
1949	6	0	2	1
1950	3	1	2	4
1922-1950	73	12	37	33

As of 1 February 1951, there were three contentious cases and one request for an advisory opinion pending before the Court.[34] Much of the work of the Court, moreover, has been devoted to the interpretation of treaties, questions of its own jurisdiction, and the functions of particular international organs. Nevertheless, in relation to its age and rate of activity, the contribution which the Court has managed to make is far from negligible. Such, at least, has been the consensus of observers who have made careful studies of the work of the Court.[35]

[33] The Court also made 137 orders. (Manley O. Hudson, *op. cit.*, p. 779.) Most of the orders dealt with procedural matters, but substantive issues of general significance were involved in some. See, *e.g.*, the orders of 19 August 1929, and 6 December 1930, in the Free Zones case, PCIJ, *Publications*, Series A, Nos. 22 and 24.

[34] For the nature of these cases, see p. 33 n. 52 and p. 77 n. 65.

[35] One of them has written a fat volume on international law containing a detailed analysis of the contributions made by the Court and by the arbitral tribunals established within the framework of the Permanent Court of Arbitration. Georg Schwarzenberger, *op. cit.*, 681 pp. See also H. Lauterpacht, *op. cit., passim;* Manley O. Hudson, *op. cit.*, pp. 628-30; Pierre Derevitzky, *Les Principes du Droit International tels qu'ils se Dégagent de la Jurisprudence de la Cour Permanente de Justice Internationale* (Paris, A. Pedone, 1932). Cf. A. Hammarskjöld, *op. cit.*, pp. 249-50, 335-55; Jean Collette, *Les Principes de Droit des Gens dans la Jurisprudence de la Cour Permanente de Justice Internationale* (Paris, Berger-Levrault, 1932), pp. 194-99.

In many fields, no discussion of international law is possible today without reference to the judgments and opinions of the Court. Among the problems with respect to which the Court has made significant contributions are, aside from questions of its own jurisdiction and procedure, those of the nature and sources of international law, the relation between international and municipal law, the nature and attributes of international legal personality, the meaning of independence of states, the status of territories under mandate, the powers and functions of international organs, the meaning of the concept of domestic jurisdiction of states, the principles of international arbitration, state succession and its effect on private interests, acquisition of sovereignty in polar regions, international waterways, exercise of criminal jurisdiction, responsibility of states and measure of damages in cases of injuries suffered by other states or their nationals, diplomatic privileges and immunities, the nature, validity, interpretation and termination of treaties, the effect of treaties on third parties and individuals, the use of force between states, and the duties of neutrals.

A few of the most recent contributions of the Court deserve special attention. Mention has already been made of the advisory opinion of the Court upholding the international personality of the United Nations and its capacity to present international claims. On the authority of the Court's opinion, action was undertaken by the United Nations to obtain reparation for the deaths and injuries of its agents in Palestine. As a result, Israel has already paid $54,628 and expressed regrets with respect to the death of Count Bernadotte, the United Nations Mediator in Palestine, and negotiations on other claims are pending.[36] The practice of states is thus already incorporating the rights and duties arising out of the legal position of the United Nations as defined by the Court.

Another recent holding of the Court, which has not drawn

---

36 For a summary of the action taken, see *United Nations Bulletin,* Vol. IX (15 November 1950), p. 578.

much notice, may yet come to be recognized as a milestone in the development of international law. In the Corfu Channel case, submitted by the United Kingdom and Albania, the Court unanimously decided that the United Kingdom had violated international law by sending its warships without the consent of Albania into Albanian territorial waters for the purpose of sweeping mines and collecting evidence bearing on the responsibility of the Albanian government for the presence of minefields in the Corfu Channel which had previously caused damage to British warships, although Albania was held responsible for the damage. In reaching this conclusion, the Court said:

> The Court can only regard the alleged right of intervention [to secure possession of evidence in the territory of another state] as the manifestation of a policy of force, such as has, in the past, given rise to most serious abuses and such as cannot, whatever be the present defects in international organization, find a place in international law. . . . The United Kingdom Agent, in his speech in reply, has further classified 'Operation Retail' among methods of self-protection or self-help. The Court cannot accept this defence either. Between independent States, respect for territorial sovereignty is an essential foundation of international relations. The Court recognizes that the Albanian Government's complete failure to carry out its duties aftter the explosions, and the dilatory nature of its diplomatic notes, are extenuating circumstances for the action of the United Kingdom Government. But to ensure respect for international law, of which it is the organ, the Court must declare that the action of the British Navy constituted a violation of Albanian sovereignty.[37]

The implications of this pronouncement are far-reaching. It is to be noted that the Court did not refer to the United Nations Charter. For the first time, the Court put the weight of its authority behind the proposition that the use of force by way of intervention or self-help in relations between states is now forbidden by general international law. The practical results of this pronouncement remain to be seen.

[37] ICJ Reports 1949, p. 35.

The Corfu Channel case also provides valuable guidance as to the right of passage through a territorial strait connecting two parts of the high seas. It may be significant that since the adjudication of this case, in which the Court held that foreign warships had the right of "innocent passage" through Albanian territorial waters in the Corfu Strait, no difficulties have arisen with respect to the use of the Strait by foreign vessels.

Factors Affecting the Performance of the Court's Law-Developing Function

The work of the Court is not perfect and has not escaped criticism. Nor has it entirely escaped the suspicion of undue political motivation – a suspicion which is discussed in some detail below. It is impossible to deal here with the merits of the varous criticisms directed at the soundness and cogency of the positions taken by the Court on specific legal questions. One general criticism appears to be justified, however. The value of the Court's work as a guide for the future, and consequently as a means of development of international law, is enhanced by full and cogent presentation of the reasoning behind its decisions. It is realized, of course, that a court may sometimes be guided in its action by considerations and feelings different from the ostensible grounds given in its opinion. Despite this often unavoidable subjective element in the functioning of a tribunal, the significance of the action taken by it within the general legal framework remains dependent on the understanding of the connection of such action with some accepted standards and techniques. Furthermore, if the reasoning given in the opinion is cogent and generally accepted as a guide for the future, its divergence from the actual motivation of the judges is not very important.

The Court has not been consistent in its apparent recognition of the importance of this factor. Many of its decisions are supported by extensive discussions which throw much-needed light on their significance. This is true, for instance, of the advisory opinion on the capacity of the United Nations to claim reparation for injuries suffered in its service, which contains a discussion of great value for the understanding of the meaning of the concept of international legal personality.[38] In other cases, however, its remarks on the standards it was applying have been so brief and sibylline as to be more productive of perplexity than of clarification. The advisory opinion on the Austro-German Customs Regime, delivered in 1931,[39] which has given rise to suspicions of political motivation, has been particularly criticized in this respect.[40] Another example is the failure of the Court in the Eastern Greenland case, decided in 1933,[41] to explain its view that an oral declaration made by the Norwegian Foreign Minister was binding on Norway, in the face of a contention by Norway that he had no constitutional power to make a commitment of that nature. The pronouncement of the Court on this point has been generally regarded as of considerable importance, but its implications have remained unclear.[42] More recently, the Court failed to indicate clearly in the Corfu Channel case how it found the law it applied. Nor has it ever made manifest the reasons for adopting certain standards of treaty interpretation.

In some cases the failure of the Court to be explicit in its reasoning is perhaps due to divergences in the approaches of the various members of the Court composing the majority on a particular issue. Insofar as the law-developing function of the Court is concerned, it might be preferable to allow the divergences to be fully exposed and presented in individual opinions of the concurring and dissenting judges.[43]

---

38 ICJ Reports 1949, p. 174.

39 PCIJ, *Publications,* Series A/B, No. 41.

40 See, *e.g.,* H. Lauterpacht, *op. cit.,* p. 20.

41 PCIJ, *Publications,* Series A/B, No. 53.

42 See, *e.g.,* Harvard Research in International Law, "Law of Treaties: Draft Convention with Comment," *American Journal of International Law,* Vol. 29 (1935), Supplement, p. 1007, and Charles Fairman, "Competence to Bind the State to an International Engagement," *American Journal of International Law,* Vol. 30 (1936), pp. 457-58.

43 The dissenting judges, who generally have not hesitated to present their

It is to be hoped that in the future the court will be fully alive to its responsibility as a law-developing agency for the cogency and explicitness of its reasoned opinions on points of law.[44]

The performance of the Court's law-developing function also depends on the members and organs of the international community which the Court serves. They must, first of all, give the Court the opportunity to function by submitting disputes or requests for opinions to it. The factors determining the number and nature of contentious cases submitted to the Court will be discussed in detail below, in Chapter III dealing with the role of the Court in the settlement of disputes, since normally a contentious case is submitted because it is desired to settle a particular dispute. The desire to obtain authoritative guidance for the future may, however, be a factor in the decision of a state or international organ to resort to the Court. This is particularly true of decisions to request advisory opinions. Such an opinion may, of course, be asked solely with a view to disposing of a pending controversy or situation. All of the requests for advisory opinions actually addressed to the Court have been suggested by concrete problems with which the requesting organs were faced, but some of them clearly envisaged the need for guidance in future situations. Thus the request for an advisory opinion on the capacity of the United Nations to make international claims for injuries to its agents was suggested by the incidents in Palestine, but it was cast in abstract terms and was designed to elicit guidance for action in all future cases of like character.[45]

---

views freely, must not, however, undermine the authority of the Court by impugning the integrity or the intelligence of the majority. Cf. Manley O. Hudson, "The Twenty-Eighth Year of the World Court," *American Journal of International Law,* Vol. 44 (1950), pp. 19-21.

44 See H. Lauterpacht, *op. cit.,* pp. 20-24.

45 See the oral statement of Dr. Ivan S. Kerno on behalf of the Secretary-General of the United Nations, Reparation for Injuries Suffered in the Service of the United Nations: ICJ Pleadings 1949, p. 69, in which the speaker dwelt at length on the importance of the Court's opinion for the development of international law and organization.

It is neither likely nor desirable that an international organ should take the trouble to ask for an opinion on general or hypothetical questions of law not suggested by an actual need for guidance. A judicial tribunal is not designed to function in a vacuum. A question on which the opinion of the Court is sought can be satisfactorily answered only if there is an element of concreteness which enables the Court to relate it to the actual development and needs of the international community. It must be sufficiently specific to be answered adequately without too many qualifications and assumptions. And preferably it should be related to some actually existing differences of opinion justifying a number of governments in going to the trouble and expense of earnestly presenting varying points of view to the Court, and thus giving it the benefit of a quasi-contentious proceeding. Furthermore, as specified in the Charter and the Statute, they must be "legal" questions, that is, capable of being adequately answered by the application of judicial techniques within the existing framework of law.[46]

The Permanent Court of International Justice helped by its advisory opinions to define the powers of several international organs, including the Council of the League and the International Labour Organisation. By 1951 the General Assembly had authorized the Economic and Social Council, the Trusteeship Council, the Interim Committee of the General Assembly, and nine specialized agencies to ask for such opinions, with some restrictions.

The possible role of advisory opinions as a device for the development of international law received clear recognition in a resolution of the General Assembly adopted on 14 November 1947, which was worded as follows:

The General Assembly,

Considering that it is a responsibility of the United Nations to encourage the progressive development of international law;

---

[46] For a further discussion of what is meant by legal disputes and questions, see pp. 71-74.

Considering that it is of paramount importance that the interpretation of the Charter of the United Nations and the constitutions of the specialized agencies should be based on recognized principles of international law;

Considering that the International Court of Justice is the principal judicial organ of the United Nations;

Considering that it is also of paramount importance that the Court should be utilized to the greatest practicable extent in the progressive development of international law, both in regard to legal issues between States and in regard to constitutional interpretation,

Recommends that organs of the United Nations and the specialized agencies should, from time to time, review the difficult and important points of law within the jurisdiction of the International Court of Justice which have arisen in the course of their activities and involve questions of principle which it is desirable to have settled, including points of law relating to the interpretation of the Charter of the United Nations or the constitutions of the specialized agencies, and, if duly authorized according to Article 96, paragraph 2, of the Charter, should refer them to the International Court of Justice for an advisory opinion.[47]

The General Assembly thus endeavored to carry out in part its task of initiating studies and making recommendations for the purpose of "encouraging the progressive development of international law and its codification." (Article 13 (1a) of the Charter)

The experience of the Court gives relatively little support to the apprehensions of early critics who questioned the propriety of endowing it with an advisory function.[48] The Court has managed to keep its judicial character, and its

---

47 Official Records of the Second Session of the General Assembly, Resolutions, 16 September-29 November 1947, p. 103; also in ICJ *Yearbook 1947-1948*, p. 19. See further, Yuen-li Liang, "Notes on Legal Questions Concerning the United Nations," *American Journal of International Law*, Vol. 42 (1948), pp. 439-44. The resolution was adopted by forty-six to six votes, with two abstentions. The opposition came from the Soviet bloc. For critical comment, see Manley O. Hudson, "The Twenty-Sixth Year of the World Court," *American Journal of International Law*, Vol. 42 (1948), pp. 15-19.

48 See, *e.g.*, John Bassett Moore, "The Question of Advisory Opinions," PCIJ, *Publications*, Series D, No. 2, pp. 383 ff., reprinted in *The Collected Papers of John Bassett Moore* (New Haven, Yale University Press, 1944),

advisory opinions have made a valuable contribution to international law. It apparently has the power to refuse to give an opinion,[49] but it cannot lightly exercise this power, and the responsibility for the nature of a question addressed to it is primarily lodged with the requesting international organ.

Among the dangers to be avoided in connection with the advisory function of the Court is the possibility of undermining the tribunal's authority as well as wasting its time. As already pointed out the prestige of the Court would be hurt, for instance, if there were frequent instances of non-compliance with its advisory opinions by the international organs or the states concerned. International organs must exercise self-restraint in addressing requests for opinions to the Court. Such restraint was probably responsible, at least in part, for the fact that the Permanent Court of International Justice escaped the imputation of failure.[50]

No international organ so far has taken action squarely in conflict with an advisory opinion given at its request. An international organ may be empowered, of course, in carrying out its political functions to take into consideration factors other than the legal relations of the states concerned as determined by the Court in an advisory opinion. In exercising this power an organ would not be showing any disregard for the legal authority of the Court. The situation would be different, however, if an organ proceeded to exer-

---

Vol. V, p. 329 ff.; but cf. his later view in John Bassett Moore, *International Law and Some Current Illusions* (New York, Macmillan Co., 1924), pp. 129-32. The advisory opinion on the Austro-German Customs Regime undoubtedly hurt the Court's prestige. See Hans Kaufmann, *Die Gutachten des Ständigen Internationalen Gerichtshofes als Mittel zwischenstaatlicher Streitschlichtung* (Basel, Helbing and Lichtenhahn, 1939), p. 228, and discussion on pp. 53-54 below.

49 "Article 65 of the Statute is permissive. It gives the Court the power to examine whether the circumstances of the case are of such a character as should lead it to decline to answer the Request." Interpretation of Peace Treaties, Advisory Opinion: ICJ Reports 1950, p. 72. Cf. Manley O. Hudson, *op. cit.*, pp. 498-501 and cases there cited.

50 Its refusal to give an advisory opinion in the Eastern Carelia case, mentioned above, probably contributed to this record. For further discussion of the policies followed in making requests for advisory opinions, see pp. 88-95 below.

cise a power which the Court had held it lacked. In such a case, there would be a direct conflict between the organ and the Court on a legal question. If an international organ is determined to assert its power to pursue a certain course of action regardless of the outcome of a request for an advisory opinion as to whether it has such power, it is better for it to refrain from making the request. Such an assertion of power, in the absence of an opinion of the Court, may itself be effective in developing international law in the direction desired by the organ concerned. The Security Council appears to have adopted this policy when it proceeded to intervene in the Indonesian situation after rejecting a proposal to submit to the Court the question of its power to do so.[51] Furthermore, an international organ should preferably not address requests for advice on substantially the same legal questions to the Court and to another agency at the same time, as the General Assembly appears to have done in 1950 in connection with the problem of reservations to multilateral treaties.[52]

The extent to which the submission of a dispute or question to the Court enables the latter to perform its law-developing function depends on the nature and scope of the

---

[51] For further discussion, see pp. 94-95.

[52] On 16 November 1950 the General Assembly approved a resolution requesting the Court to give an advisory opinion on the legal effects of reservations to the Genocide Convention and inviting the International Law Commission (set up by the General Assembly for the purpose of progressive development and codification of international law) to study the question of reservations to multilateral conventions "both from the point of view of codification and from that of the progressive development of international law" and to report thereon to the General Assembly. Resolutions Adopted by the General Assembly During the Period 19 September to 15 December 1950 (General Assembly, Official Records: Fifth Session, Supplement No. 20), p. 74. Theoretically, this resolution made possible the expression of inconsistent views by the Court and by the Commission as to what is the existing law on the subject. It is to be hoped that the Commission will refrain from taking a position inconsistent with that of the Court, since the Court's opinion should be available to the Commission before the completion of the latter's study. The preferable course would have been for the General Assembly to have obtained an opinion from the Court on the specific question relating to the Genocide Convention before submitting the general question to the International Law Commission. The General Assembly would then have been in a better position to determine the precise nature of the task referred to the Commission.

issues, the terms in which they are framed, and the skill and completeness with which they are developed and clarified by the interested parties in their pleadings and arguments. A dispute in which the Court has to deal solely with issues of fact is obviously not productive of opportunities for the development of substantive standards of international law. The Court has little power to take part in the framing of the issues before it, since its jurisdiction rests on voluntary submission. The terms and scope of requests for advisory opinions contained in resolutions adopted by such representative bodies as the General Assembly may bear the unavoidable marks of compromises and hasty preparation.[53] The necessity for compromise may also affect the formulation of the terms of reference reached by agreement between two or more states. The Court has not hesitated to correct linguistic ineptness in the terms of questions submitted to it for advisory opinions.[54]

The procedure and practice of the Court give ample opportunities to the interested parties for the careful preparation and presentation of their contentions. It is unnecessary here to discuss the quality of the actual pleadings and arguments in the various cases before the Court. Special mention should be made, however, of the statements on behalf of the Secretary-General of the United Nations sub-

---

53 The decision of the General Assembly to refer the problem of reservations to multilateral treaties to both the Court and the International Law Commission was apparently the result of a compromise between those who would refer it to the Court and those who wanted the Commission alone to study it.

54 See Advisory Opinion on Competence of the International Labor Organization with Respect to Agricultural Production, PCIJ, *Publications,* Series B, Nos. 2 and 3, p. 59; Advisory Opinion on Interpretation of the Greco-Turkish Agreement of 1 December 1926, PCIJ, *Publications,* Series B, No. 16, p. 15. In the advisory opinion on Reparation for Injuries Suffered in the Service of the United Nations, where the Court had to deal with questions referring in terms to "an international claim against the responsible *de jure* or *de facto* government," it stated that it understood the questions to be directed to claims against a *state,* and that it would, therefore, in the opinion, use the expression "state" or "defendant state." ICJ Reports 1949, p. 177. It thus brought the wording of the request into conformity with the principle that states, and not governments, are the subjects of international law.

mitted to the Court in advisory proceedings. These statements, prepared by the Legal Department of the Secretariat, are generally of a very high quality and are bound to be of assistance to the Court in clarifying the issues and finding the law.

One of the subsidiary functions of the pleadings and arguments before the Court is to assist in the understanding of the import of the Court's decisions, particularly in cases where the reasoning given in the opinions delivered by the Court and its individual members is not entirely adequate for that purpose. The regular publication of the pleadings, arguments and statements — a practice which the new Court inherited from the old — is, therefore, of some importance in the performance by the Court of its law-developing function.

Although the law-developing function of the Court is closely and indissolubly linked with the function of disposing of particular controversies, the two are not identical and may occasionally conflict. This might be true, for instance, if the parties empowered the Court — as they are apparently permitted to do by the Statute — to decide a dispute *ex aequo et bono* without regard to legal standards. The dispute might be effectively disposed of, but the Court might be deprived of an opportunity to interpret and apply the law.

Furthermore, should the number of cases submitted to the Court increase, the resulting pressure on its time might prevent it from giving thorough consideration to the long-range implications of some of its decisions and might also make less likely the preparation of fully reasoned opinions. It must be remembered that the Court is administering a legal system which is, in many respects, vague and incomplete. The proper development of such a system often calls for more deliberation and more study than are necessary for the administration of the highly developed legal systems of modern states. The history of mixed claims commissions indicates that when thousands of international claims have to be disposed of within a few years less care may be employed in the presentation and consideration of the legal issues and in the preparation of reasoned opinions than when an arbitrator has to deal with only one dispute. When the primary function of a tribunal is to put an end to a large number of controversies, "expeditiousness of adjudication is of prime importance."[55]

In modern states the conflict between the law-developing and the decision-making functions has been generally alleviated by the creation of hierarchies of courts, with the lower tribunals adjudicating all controversies brought before them and the courts of last resort primarily exercising the power of review in cases which involve questions of law transcending in importance the interests of the parties immediately concerned.[56]

Should the pressure of work on the Court greatly increase, consideration will have to be given to relieving it by dividing the Court into chambers for speedier adjudication of the less important cases, or by creating regional or circuit international tribunals for the same purpose.[57] Normally cases are heard and decided, and opinions given by the full Court, although one or more judges may be dispensed from sitting, as provided by the Rules. A quorum of nine judges suffices to constitute the Court. A chamber of five judges which is formed annually may hear and determine cases by summary procedure, and the Court is also empowered to form special chambers for dealing with particular cases and categories of cases. The special chambers are used at the request of the parties. However, during the existence of the Permanent Court of International Justice only two disputes, both arising out of differences between Bulgaria and Greece concerning the interpretation of the Treaty of Neuilly, were referred

[55] A. H. Feller, *The Mexican Claims Commissions 1923-1934* (New York, Macmillian Co., 1935), p. 318.

[56] In this connection, see *e.g.*, Rule 38 (5) of the Supreme Court of the United States indicating the character of reasons which will be considered by the Supreme Court in passing upon petitions for review of decisions of lower courts on *writ of certiorari.*

[57] It may be noted that a Central American Court of Justice existed between 1907-1917 and that proposals have been made and studied for the establishment of an Inter-American Court of Justice.

to the chamber for summary procedure, and the other chambers remained entirely without business; in the new Court there has been as yet no resort to any of the chambers.

The Charter of the United Nations refers to the Court as "the *principal* judicial organ of the United Nations," thus not precluding the possibility of existence of subsidiary judicial organs under United Nations auspices. In the period between the two world wars states resorted extensively to arbitral tribunals of various types, and this practice undoubtedly helped to keep down the volume of litigation in the Court. The states are free to do so again. Some of the arbitration clauses now in force provide for appeals from the decisions of the arbitrators to the Court. Techniques for properly apportioning the workload of international adjudication between the Court and lower international tribunals will be undoubtedly developed as needed.

The Court's Law-Developing Activity and Peace

The extent to which the law-developing activity of the Court has in fact contributed to the maintenance of international peace and security by reducing friction between states and enabling them to cooperate more effectively is not capable of appraisal. As already noted, after the decision in the Corfu Channel case no difficulties have arisen in connection with the use of the Corfu Strait by foreign vessels, but it would be rash to attribute this entirely to the influence of the Court. Similarly, it is impossible to estimate the extent to which the Court's contribution to the definiteness of international law standards in other fields has in fact tended to reduce international tensions. It cannot even be said with assurance that the capacity to make international claims, which the Court found the United Nations to possess, has facilitated the performance by the United Nations of its security functions.

The growth of the "seamless web of law" is often slow and its immediate effects not apparent. Yet no stable society and no legal system giving reasonable assurance of general peace and security are conceivable without it. The law-developing work of the Court has barely started. It is a promise rather than a fulfillment. But the creation and successful functioning of a standing international tribunal has introduced a new and potentially powerful factor in the shaping of international law. It is a start in the right direction.

III. THE COURT AND THE SETTLEMENT OF DISPUTES

Despite the existence of a pattern of generally recognized standards of conduct, states, like individuals, often find their interests clashing with those of the other members of the community. In the absence of a superior authority with the power to settle such conflicts and enforce the settlements, states have often been tempted and have in fact resorted to violence. The development of techniques for the peaceful settlement or adjustment of disputes between states has long been regarded as an essential condition of the maintenance of international peace and security. The Charter proclaims that to the end of achieving its first purpose, the maintenance of international peace and security, the United Nations is "to bring about by peaceful means, and in conformity with the principles of justice and international law, adjustment or settlement of international disputes or situations which might lead to a breach of the peace." (Article 1 (1)) All Members of the United Nations undertake to "settle their international disputes by peaceful means in such a manner that international peace and security, and justice, are not endangered." (Article 2 (3))

The accent in the Charter is thus on the peaceful settlement of disputes which, if allowed to remain unsettled, might endanger international peace and security. In a broader sense, however, every unsettled dispute between states contributes to international friction, and every successful settlement of a controversy by peaceful means strengthens the structure of international peace and security. Furthermore, every instance of a successful resort to peaceful methods of settlement may contribute to the development of a habit and tradition, making resort to violence less likely in future controversies. In this sense the peaceful settlement of every dispute, however minor, is connected with the achievement of the first purpose of the United Nations.

Although the political organs of the United Nations have the function of providing by recommendation for the peaceful settlement of any dispute which might endanger the maintenance of international peace and security, Article 33 of the Charter imposes upon the parties to such a dispute the duty "first of all" to "seek a solution by negotiation, enquiry, mediation, conciliation, arbitration, judicial settlement, resort to regional agencies or arrangements, or other peaceful means of their own choice." This Article enumerates most of the means of peaceful settlement of international disputes that have been actually used by states. Negotiation is obviously the first method to which states normally resort when they have a disagreement. Enquiry, mediation and conciliation are all methods in which recourse is had to a third state, a body such as a commission, or an individual, to help the parties arrive at a mutually acceptable solution. In all of these procedures the termination of the dispute normally depends upon the voluntary acceptance by all the parties of the proposed terms of settlement.

Arbitration and judicial settlement, on the other hand, normally refer to the termination of a dispute by a decision which the parties accept in advance as binding (although arbitrators may also be empowered to make recommendations without binding effect). "Judicial settlement" has in practice come to mean settlement by the decision of a standing international tribunal such as the Court, while "arbitration" is generally used to describe a procedure leading to a settlement by the decision of an individual or body specially appointed to pass on a specific dispute or set of disputes between two or more states. Normally, the arbitrators are selected by the parties. Since the jurisdiction of the Court, no less than that of arbitral tribunals, depends in principle on the voluntary submission of the parties, what has been gained by the Court's establishment?

Some of the reasons which inspired the early proponents of the creation of a standing international court were set forth in the instructions of Secretary of State Elihu Root to the United States delegation at the Hague Conference of 1907:

> There can be no doubt that the principal objection to arbitration rests not upon the unwillingness of nations to submit their controversies to impartial arbitration, but upon an apprehension that the arbitrations to which they submit may not be impartial. It has been a very general practice for arbitrators to act, not as judges deciding questions of fact and law upon the record before them under a sense of judicial responsibility, but as negotiators effecting settlements of the questions brought before them in accordance with the traditions and usages and subject to all the considerations and influences which affect diplomatic agents. The two methods are radically different, proceed upon different standards of honorable obligation, and frequently lead to widely differing results. It very frequently happens that a nation which would be very willing to submit its differences to an impartial judicial determination is unwilling to subject them to this kind of diplomatic process. . . . It should be your effort to bring about in the Second Conference a development of The Hague Tribunal into a permanent tribunal composed of judges who are judicial officers and nothing else, who are paid adequate salaries, who have no other occupation, and who will devote their entire time to the trial and decision of international causes by judicial methods and under a sense of judicial responsibility. These judges should be so selected from the different countries that the different systems of law and procedure and the principal languages shall be fairly represented. The court should be made of such dignity, consideration, and rank that the best and ablest jurists will accept appointment to it, and that the whole world will have absolute confidence in its judgments.[1]

The real reason why states are often unwilling to submit their disputes to arbitration may not always be that stated by Root, but it is evident that the Court as instituted in 1922 and reinstituted in 1946 largely meets the requirements laid down by him.

The creation of the Court was not intended to prevent and has not, in fact, deterred states and international organs from resorting to arbitral tribunals of their own choice. Thousands of claims were adjudicated during the interwar period

---

[1] Green H. Hackworth, *Digest of International Law* (Washington, Government Printing Office, 1943), Vol. VI, pp. 61-62.

by the mixed arbitral tribunals set up under the treaties of peace; other thousands were submitted to the mixed claims commissions set up under agreements between Mexico and six other states, and between Panama and the United States; and many other cases were adjudicated by arbitral tribunals established within and without the framework of the Permanent Court of Arbitration.[2]

The fact that the creation and the activity of an arbitral tribunal are subject to the complete control of the parties to the dispute has many advantages. It enables the parties to select as arbitrators persons or bodies in whom they repose special confidence, or who have special knowledgc and skills.[3] The parties also determine the place of the tribunal's work. The control of procedure by the parties may permit the prompt disposal of minor claims by summary action, and may considerably reduce the expenses of the proceedings. The parties, moreover, are free to prescribe the standards by which the arbitrators are to be guided; under the guise of adjudication they may provide for settlement by a binding decision of a political nature, that is, one based on such considerations as the relative power of the parties or the necessity for assuaging popular passions in one or both of them. The fact that arbitration has sometimes been used for this purpose has led to a tendency on the part of some arbitrators to feel that they are justified in assuming the powers of mediators rather than judges, even in the absence of indications that such was the desire of the parties.[4] Furtheremore, political considerations have unavoidably entered into the selection of the arbitrators by the parties.

---

2 The three volumes of *Reports of International Arbitral Awards*, prepared by the Registry of the Court and published in 1948-1949 by the United Nations, contain fifty-nine cases decided during the interwar period by tribunals other than the mixed arbitral trbunals and mixed claims commissions.

3 This may be of importance in the settlement of disputes of a highly technical character, such as those arising between postal or railway administrations or in the fields of telecommunications and civil aviation.

4 See, *e.g.*, the views of Lieber, first umpire in the claims commission established under the convention of 1868 between Mexico and the United States, John Bassett Moore, *History and Digest of International Arbitrations*

Distinguishing Characteristics of the Court

The establishment of the Court has thus provided the international community with a method of settling disputes by binding decision which has both advantages and disadvantages in comparison with the process of international arbitration. The distinguishing characteristics of the Court may be analyzed as those of the standards and techniques applied in the settlement of disputes, and those of organization, composition and facilities.

Standards and Techniques

The standards and techniques normally applied by the Court are those of international law. Article 38 of the Statute reads as follows:

1. The Court, whose function is to decide in accordance with international law such disputes as are submitted to it, shall apply:

a. international conventions, whether general or particular, establishing rules expressly recognized by the contesting states;

b. international custom, as evidence of a general practice accepted as law;

c. the general principles of law recognized by civilized nations;

d. subject to the provisions of Article 59, judicial decisions and the teachings of the most highly qualified publicists of the various nations, as subsidiary means for the determination of rules of law.

2. This provision shall not prejudice the power of the Court to decide a case *ex aequo et bono*, if the parties agree thereto.

As has been already explained, international law is a pattern of standards of conduct worked out and generally

to Which the United States Has Been a Party (Washington, Government Printing Office, 1898), Vol. II, p. 1301 n.; and articles by Clifton J. Child and William Cullen Dennis on "The Venezuela-British Guiana Boundary Arbitration of 1899," *American Journal of International Law*, Vol. 44 (1950), pp. 682 and 720.

accepted by the international community through practice and express or tacit consensus. Since this pattern has the same general function — regulation of relations among the members and organs of the community — as law in the more highly organized communities, and since it has been found convenient in practice to treat it as a system of law, the advantages of the application of its standards to particular controversies by methods and techniques similar to those employed by the judicial organs of modern states have long been recognized. Arbitral tribunals set up by the parties to a dispute have often applied the standards of international law by such methods and techniques. The Court, like other tribunals, in applying general standards to particular cases, unavoidably refines, develops and even changes the content of such standards. On this fact is based, as already noted in the preceding chapter, its law-developing function.

Nevertheless, a judicial tribunal is expected normally to remain in its decisions within the general framework of the system of law it is administering and to attach great weight to the impersonal character and uniformity of the standards it is applying. The advantages of uniformity and predictability, though these may never be absolute, are among the fundamental reasons for the existence of legal standards, since in their absence no member of the community would have reasonable assurance as to how he should be treated, how he is expected to behave, and what the consequences of certain actions are likely to be. Application of the standards by a tribunal is a sanction of their observance in practice. Normally, moreover, the impersonal application of fairly definite pre-existing standards is generally felt to be just. Application of known standards is most likely to result in the fulfillment of reasonable expectations, and is thus conducive to stability and security. These are the basic reasons why legal standards of conduct have the double function of guiding the members of the community in their activities and also normally serving as the criteria by which disputes arising out of such activities are settled.

It must be noted, however, that the Court, like arbitral tribunals, may be empowered by agreement between the parties to look beyond the existing specific standards of international law for criteria to be applied in the settlement of a particular dispute. This is the apparent significance of Article 38 (2). Since the Court has never had the occasion to interpret this provision, no states having ever agreed to invoke it, its precise meaning is still uncertain. There may be a tendency to interpret it restrictively; but there is wide agreement among the writers that it gives the Court a latitude which it otherwise would not have. Furthermore, since the Court, under Article 38 (1a) of the Statute, is required to apply the rules established by treaty between the parties, the latter may have the power to prescribe for the settlement of their dispute standards other than those of general international law.[5] The Court, moreover, may modify its rules of procedure on the joint proposal of the parties;[6] and the dispute, by agreement of the parties, may be referred to the chamber for summary procedure or to a special chamber. The parties, therefore, are actually in the position jointly to exercise some control over the standards and procedure applied by the Court.

In this respect the difference between the Court and arbitral tribunals may not seem to be very great. It is, nevertheless, of importance. The Court is more universally regarded as primarily an organ for the administration of international law, rather than of considerations of mere fairness and expediency, than are arbitral tribunals, even though many of the latter are also called upon to apply international law. It is, indeed, very doubtful that the Court would consent to serve as the means of a purely political settlement in the guise of a judicial proceeding, even if the parties agreed thereto.

---

5 See Manley O. Hudson, *The Permanent Court of International Justice 1920-1942* (New York, Macmillan Co., 1943), pp. 601-03, 618-21; H. Lauterpacht, *The Function of Law in the International Community* (Oxford, The Clarendon Press, 1933), pp. 313-29. The question whether this power has any limits has never been decided by the Court.

6 ICJ, Rules of Court, Art. 31; see also Manley O. Hudson, *op. cit.*, pp. 549-51.

As explained in the preceding chapter, the Court is better able than arbitral tribunals, owing to its continuity, to develop a body of case law. The reliance of the Court on its own precedents enhances the uniformity and impersonality of the standards applied by it.

Organization, Composition and Facilities

The Court's procedure, prescribed by the Statute and further elaborated in the Rules which the Court is empowered to make for itself,[7] is designed to assure to the parties full and equal opportunity to present and develop their respective contentions by steps very similar to those followed in the proceedings before the judicial tribunals of modern states. Cases are brought before the Court by a written application or by the notification of a special agreement. The written proceedings consist of the communication to the Court and to the parties of memorials, counter-memorials, and, if necessary, replies and rejoinders submitted by the parties with all supporting papers and documents, in the order and within the time limits fixed by the Court. The oral proceedings consist of the hearing by the Court of witnesses and experts, and of agents, counsel and advocates of the parties arguing issues of fact and of law. The Court acts by majority vote; in case of a tie the President or, in his absence, the Vice President (both elected by the Court for three-year terms), or, in the absence of both the President and the Vice President, the senior judge present casts the deciding vote.

The deliberations of the judges take place in private, but the judgment is read in open court. In the event of dispute as to the meaning or scope of the judgment, the Court construes it at the request of any party. Proceedings leading to advisory opinions are in substance similar to those in contentious cases, with the interested states being permitted to

[7] See Chapters III and IV of the Statute, and Rules of Court; also, Manley O. Hudson, *op. cit.*, pp. 537-97.

present written and oral statements and to comment on the statements made by other states or organizations.

The Court is designed to be properly equipped for dealing with questions of fact as well as of law. Not only is provision made for the production of evidence and the testimony of witnesses and experts before the Court, but the latter may entrust any individual or organization with the task of carrying out an enquiry or giving an expert opinion. The Court in its discretion may sit and exercise its functions elsewhere than at The Hague, and the special chambers may do so with the consent of the parties. Members of the Court may visit any place to which a case relates. Provision is made for the appointment of assessors to sit with the Court without the right to vote, to assist the Court in dealing with technical questions.[8]

In the Corfu Channel case the Court had to pass on complicated issues of fact. Numerous witnesses were called by both parties, much documentary evidence was produced, and the Court entrusted to a specially appointed committee of three experts the task of giving an expert opinion. These experts visited several localities adjacent to the scene of the incident, filed two reports, and were questioned by members of the Court. At a later stage of the proceedings, other experts were appointed by the Court to examine the claim for damages submitted by the British government. After these experts had filed their report, they were likewise questioned by members of the Court.[9]

Reference has already been made in the preceding chapter to the advantages of the continuous functioning of the Court and of the facilities at its disposal. The fact that the Court's existence and composition do not depend on an agreement between the parties to a dispute may save the time and effort that might otherwise be required for negotiating such an agreement. More important, however, is the effect that the

[8] On assessors, see the Statute, Art. 30 (2); also, Manley O. Hudson, *op. cit.*, pp. 348-49, and "The Twenty-Fourth Year of the World Court," *American Journal of International Law*, Vol. 40 (1946), p. 28.

[9] ICJ Reports 1949, pp. 4, 8-9, 13-15, 244, 247.

organization and composition of the Court may have on the confidence of the international community in the impartiality, thoroughness and ability with which it performs its tasks, and consequently on the readiness of states to submit their differences to it.

It is clear, of course, that this effect may not be the same in all cases. A government which has a weak case and would prefer to rely on its political power may be actually deterred from going to the Court if it knows that political influence will be unavailing there. A government which sincerely believes in the merits of its case is normally more willing to submit it to a tribunal whose impartiality, thoroughness and ability it trusts. A government which knows that its case is weak and is willing to admit it but prevented from so doing by domestic political pressures may be inclined to rely on the authority of the Court for escape from an unpleasant dilemma. The authority and prestige of the Court, moreover, lend greater strength and stability to a settlement based on its decision.[10]

The prestige of a judicial tribunal depends not only on its impartiality, but also on the skill and conscientiousness with which its tasks are performed, and on the professional and personal standing of its members. The Court is expected to give careful and thorough consideration to the issues on which it has to pass. The relatively small number of cases submitted each year to the Court enables it to live up to a high standard of thoroughness, even if the conciseness of some of its opinions does not always make this evident.[11] The reputation of the Court has been enhanced by the professional standing of its members, most of whom, prior to their elevation to the international Bench, had distinguished themselves as scholars, judges, or legal advisers to governments, and had acquired wide renown. Their opinions on

---

10 See p. 74.

11 For procedures followed by the Court in its deliberations and in the drafting of its opinions, see Manley O. Hudson, *The Permanent Court of International Justice 1920-1942*, pp. 579-83.

legal matters would be accorded weight even if not backed by the official authority of the Court.[12]

Injudicious behavior on the part of the members of the Court may affect its prestige unfavorably. It has been pointed out, for example, that the unrestrained strictures on the Court's views contained in some recent dissenting opinions may have disastrous effects on the tribunal's authority.[13] In 1950 the Soviet judge, S. B. Krylov, exposed himself to criticism in the Security Council by appearing to prejudge in a published article some of the legal issues arising out of the conflict in Korea which might conceivably come before the Court.[14]

Impartiality

Judges are human beings who, as such, are unavoidably influenced by emotions. They are, furthermore, products of definite cultural environments. No matter how conscientiously a judge endeavors to perform his task, he cannot be anybody but himself. In fact, his endeavor to be a good and impartial judge is itself based on an emotional drive determined largely by cultural conditioning. Nevertheless, particular judges succeed in differing degrees in approaching the generally accepted ideal of impartiality.

The impartiality of the members of an international tribunal is always somewhat suspect because national and traditional loyalties are felt to be among the strongest of emotions, and also because the political interests of particular states unavoidably enter into the selection of such members. Both of these considerations have been taken into account in the provisions of the Statute dealing with the election of the judges of the Court. The electors are directed to bear in mind not only the individual qualifications of the candi-

---

12 For biographies, see Manley O. Hudson, *op. cit.*, pp. 259-64, and ICJ *Yearbook* 1946-1947, pp. 42 ff.

13 Manley O. Hudson, "The Twenty-Eighth Year of the World Court," *American Journal of International Law*, Vol. 44 (1950), pp. 18-21.

14 See the remarks of Sir Gladwyn Jebb, Security Council, Official Records, 5th Year, No. 31, 489th Meeting, 22 August 1950, p. 20.

dates, "but also that in the body as a whole the representation of the main forms of civilization and of the principal legal systems of the world should be assured." (Article 9 of the Statute) The number of the members of the Court (fifteen) and the prohibition against any two members of the Court being of the same nationality, contained in Article 3 of the Statute,[15] may be expected to permit the various legal traditions to be represented and to minimize the possible effects of the national sympathies and traditions of the judges on the outcome of a particular proceeding, since there is likely to be a substantial number of judges having no direct connection with any of the parties. Furthermore, the possible effect of national bias is designed to be counteracted in part by the appointment of judges *ad hoc* by the parties whose nationals do not otherwise sit on the Court.[16]

The members of the Court are elected by the political organs of the United Nations composed of representatives of states, but the effect of political considerations in the elections is designed to be somewhat weakened by the provision that the candidates are to be nominated by the "national groups" composing the Permanent Court of Arbitration, or, in the case of Members of the United Nations not represented on that court, by groups specially appointed in the same way as the "national groups" of the Permanent Court of Arbitration are appointed.[17] Article 6 of the Statute con-

[15] Special provision is made for cases of dual nationality. As of 1 February 1951, the membership of the Court was divided as follows by regions and nationalities: Western Europe (Belgium, France, Norway, United Kingdom) —4; Eastern Europe (Poland, USSR, Yugoslavia) —3; Latin America (Brazil, Chile, El Salvador, Mexico) —4; Canada and the United States—2; Middle East (Egypt) —1; Far East (China) —1. It is apparent that the number of judges from Asian countries is disproportionately small.

[16] Several parties in the same interest are reckoned as one party. The Rules and practice of the Court have permitted since 1927 the appointment of judges *ad hoc* not only in contentious cases, but also in advisory proceedings related to existing disputes or questions actually pending between states. Manley O. Hudson, *The Permanent Court of International Justice 1920-1942,* pp. 361-62; Rules of Court (1946), Art. 83. For a criticism of the provision for judges *ad hoc,* see H. Lauterpacht, *The Function of Law in the International Community,* pp. 220-36.

[17] Article 44 of the Hague Convention of 1907 for the Pacific Settlement of International Disputes provides: "Each contracting Power selects four

tains a recommendation that before making the nominations each national group should "consult its highest court of justice, its legal faculties and schools of law, and its national academies and national sections of international academies devoted to the study of law." Under Article 5, each "national group" may nominate up to four persons, but not more than two of them may be of the nationality of the nominating group, and the number of candidates nominated by a group may not be more than double the number of seats to be filled. The judges are elected for nine-year terms by the General Assembly and the Security Council, and may be reelected. To provide for continuity of membership the elections are held at three-year intervals, five seats being filled at a time.[18] In these elections no state has a veto; an absolute majority of votes in the General Assembly and the Security Council is sufficient for the election of a member of the Court. If the requisite majority is not obtainable in the General Assembly or in the Security Council by the procedures specified in the Statute, the elected members of the Court fill the vacant seats from among the candidates who have obtained votes in the General Assembly or the Security Council.

These provisions have been criticized as not going far enough to make the selection of the judges independent of political influences; it has also been contended that the independence of the Court would be better safeguarded if its members were elected for life rather than for nine-year

---

persons at the most, of known competency in questions of international law, of the highest moral reputation, and disposed to accept the duties of arbitrator. . . . Two or more Powers may agree on the selection in common of one or more members. The same person can be selected by different Powers. . . ." The persons selected under this provision are members of the Permanent Court of Arbitration; those selected by each party to the Convention constitute a "national group" within the meaning of the Statute of the International Court.

18 To make this possible, the members of the Court elected in 1946 were, as provided in Article 13 of the Statute, divided by lot into three groups of five, the terms of the judges in each group expiring respectively in three, six and nine years. Under the old Statute the terms of all judges expired simultaneously.

terms.[19] Criticisms of this character appear in part to be counsels of perfection. Every court is an organ of the community it serves, and as such cannot, and probably should not, escape all connection with the political processes of the community. Even in the best organized states, judges are either appointed by political organs or elected by the people, sometimes for a term of years. Life tenure does have the effect of making a judge more independent of short-range political influences. The ultimate control of every court, however, must rest with the community. Otherwise, a court may lose touch with the needs of the community and misconceive its long-range policies. In this sense, no court can or should be absolutely independent.[20]

The impartiality and independence of the Court are further sought to be assured by provisions for the non-participation of a judge in the decision of a case with which he had been previously connected in another capacity (Article 17 of the Statute) and for the freedom of the judges from political or administrative functions and from other professional occupations (Article 16). The judges are paid adequate annual salaries (fixed in 1946 at 54,000 florins, with special allowances for the President and Vice President) and travel expenses.

There can be little doubt that the Court has greater political independence than most arbitral tribunals whose members are selected by the parties to the dispute. The members of the Court sit not as representatives of particular states, but as judges elected by organs of the world community.[21]

To what extent has the Court actually lived up to the ideal of judicial impartiality? Its general reputation has been good; as already mentioned, it was regarded as among the

---

19 Hans Kelsen, *The Law of the United Nations* (New York, Frederick A. Praeger Inc., 1950), pp. 466-75. Cf. H. Lauterpacht, *The Function of Law in the International Community,* pp. 237-41.

20 See further pp. 57-58.

21 It is of interest to note that in 1950 the Soviet member of the Court continued to sit with his Chinese colleague while in the International Law Commission, also composed of individual experts, the Soviet member withdrew in protest against the continued participation of the Chinese member.

more successful institutions of the League system. Before and during the drafting of the Charter of the United Nations, in the discussion of the question whether the Permanent Court of International Justice should be retained in the United Nations as an already existing institution or replaced by a formally new tribunal, "no dissatisfaction with the Permanent Court was voiced at any time, either at Washington or at San Francisco. Nor was any criticism expressed of its record in dealing with the cases brought before it." The record of the old Court was praised in many public statements and reports.[22] The decision to institute a new Court was not based on any dissatisfaction with the work of the old tribunal, but on the desire to make the Court an organ of the United Nations and facilitate the corresponding changes in the Statute. The structure and powers of the Court were but little affected by these changes.

The Court has not been entirely free, however, from imputations of partiality and political motivation. Its advisory opinion on the Austro-German Customs Regime, given in 1931,[23] has been particularly criticized. In this opinion, the Court held, by eight votes to seven, that a customs union between Austria and Germany, as provided for in an agreement between the two countries, would not be compatible with an agreement made by Austria in 1922 with Great Britain, France, Italy and Czechoslovakia, to which Spain and Belgium acceded, in which she had undertaken not to alienate her independence and to abstain "from any economic or financial engagement calculated directly or indirectly to compromise this independence." The customs union agreement was a matter of grave concern to the French government. The question of the compatibility of the engagements was submitted to the Council of the League by the British government and referred to the Court by the Council. Statements upholding the view that the agreements were incompatible were filed with the Court by the French,

---

22 See Manley O. Hudson, "The Twenty-Fourth Year of the World Court," *op. cit.*, p. 7.

23 PCIJ, *Publications*, Series A/B, No. 41.

Italian and Czechoslovak governments. The majority in the Court was composed of the French, Colombian, Cuban, Italian, Polish, Rumanian, Salvadoran and Spanish judges, while the United States, Belgian, British, Chinese, Dutch, German and Japanese judges dissented. It has been alleged that the line-up in the Court roughly corresponded to a "Latin" bloc and a "Teutonic" bloc. Furthermore, the reasoning of the majority was not very explicit or persuasive. Observers have pointed out, however, that a rather convincing argument in defense of the Court's integrity can be made.[24]

It is generally true that the various members of the Court and especially judges *ad hoc* "have usually supported the contentions of the governments of which they were nationals or by which they were appointed,"[25] although there have been numerous exceptions.[26] It must be remembered, moreover, that direct national interest in the outcome of a particular case is not the only possible cause of partiality. No member of the Court has ever been accused of being swayed by considerations of personal gain, but sympathy for a particular group of states or their political and social institutions may have influenced some judges. Furthermore, it is not improbable that some judges have been inclined to favor the historical legal positions or interests of their own states even in cases in which these states were not parties. It would be

---

24 See Grant Gilmore, "The International Court of Justice," *Yale Law Journal,* Vol. 55 (1946), pp. 1056-58 (where the Cuban judge is mistakenly referred to as "Brazilian") and literature there cited; Manley O. Hudson, *The Permanent Court of International Justice 1920-1942,* pp. 360 and 657; Philip C. Jessup, "The Customs Union Advisory Opinion," *American Journal of International Law,* Vol. 26 (1932), p. 105. For other literature on the case, see bibliography in Manley O. Hudson, ed., *World Court Reports,* Vol. II, p. 712. Two days before the advisory opinion was handed down the German and Austrian governments announced their intention to drop the proposed union.

25 Manley O. Hudson, *The Permanent Court of International Justice 1920-1942,* p. 355; see also H. Lauterpacht, *The Function of Law in the International Community,* pp. 230-32 and 237.

26 For a detailed analysis of the positions of the judges in particular cases in relation to their nationality, see Manley O. Hudson, *op. cit.,* pp. 355-60.

unrealistic to deny, for example, that some bias of this character may have entered into the positions taken by some judges on questions arising out of the Versailles peace settlement or out of the clashes of policy between the Soviet bloc and the Western nations.

Despite the inclination shown by many members of the Court to take a favorable attitude toward the contentions and interests of their own states or of states in similar positions, the Court apparently continues to enjoy a large measure of respect in the international community, perhaps because it is realized that the ideal of absolute impartiality is hardly ever attained even in the judicial tribunals of the best organized modern states. Governments on the losing side of the disputes or questions brought before the Court generally refrain from impugning the integrity of its motives. This has been true even of the governments in the Soviet bloc.

The Court as a whole has certainly been much more conscious of its responsibilities as a truly international organ than have been the organs composed of governmental representatives. The national loyalties of its members have tended to cancel each other. Some members of the Court, moreover, have displayed readiness to disregard the positions of their own governments, as a few examples will show. In the first contentious case decided by the Permanent Court of International Justice, the *S.S. Wimbledon,* the claim of the British, French, Italian and Japanese governments that Germany had violated the Treaty of Versailles by barring passage through the Kiel Canal to a French ship carrying munitions to Poland, then at war with Russia, was upheld by the Court, but the Italian judge, Dionisio Anzilotti, was one of the three judges who dissented.[27] Apparently this is the only contentious case in which a judge found himself in a minority opposing the position of his own state. The cases in which judges have joined majorities against the positions taken by their own states are more frequent. The most re-

---

[27] PCIJ, *Publications,* Series A, No. 1.

cent contentious proceeding in which this happened was the Corfu Channel case, in which the British judge, Sir Arnold McNair, joined in the unanimous holding that the United Kingdom had violated the sovereignty of Albania by sending its warships to sweep mines in Albanian territorial waters without the consent of Albania.[28]

In advisory proceedings, where the lines between the positions of the various interested states may be less sharply drawn, divergences between the views of particular judges and the positions of their respective governments are also not infrequent. Fifteen of the thirty-three advisory opinions given by the Court were unanimous. The Canadian judge dissented from the advisory opinion on Conditions of Admission of a State to Membership in the United Nations, although the Court's opinion supported the position taken by the Canadian government.[29] In the advisory opinion on the Interpretation of Peace Treaties with Bulgaria, Hungary and Rumania (Second Phase), the United States and British judges joined the majority in rejecting the view of the United States and the United Kingdom that the Secretary-General of the United Nations was authorized to appoint the third member of a treaty commission under the peace treaties if one party failed to appoint its representative.[30]

It is of particular interest that the judges of the nationalities of the Communist-dominated states have not on all occasions taken positions most favorable to the contentions of such states. For example, the Soviet, Polish and Yugoslav judges joined the majority which upheld the jurisdiction of the Court in the Corfu Channel case against the objections of Albania, although the judge *ad hoc* (a Czech) appointed

---

28 ICJ Reports 1949, pp. 4 and 36.

29 ICJ Reports 1948, pp. 57 and 82; *Conditions of Admission of a State to Membership in the United Nations (Article 4 of the Charter)*, ICJ Pleadings 1948, pp. 18-19.

30 ICJ Reports 1950, p. 221; see statements of the United Kingdom government and the United States government, ICJ Distr. 50/13, pp. 48 and 70-71, and Distr. 50/171; also, criticism of the opinion by a representative of the United States in the General Assembly, Department of State *Bulletin*, Vol. 23, 23 October 1950, pp. 667-68.

by Albania dissented.[31] In the judgment on the merits of the case, the Polish and Yugoslav judges and the judge *ad hoc* appointed by Albania apparently concurred in the holding that Albanian sovereignty had not been violated by the peaceful passage of British warships (as distinguished from the subsequent British minesweeping operation) through Albanian territorial waters in the Corfu Strait without the consent of Albania, while the Soviet judge, as well as the Brazilian, dissented. The Polish and Yugoslav judges concurred in the judgment assessing the amount of compensation, from which the Soviet judge and the judge *ad hoc* appointed by Albania dissented.[32] None of the judges from the Communist-dominated states have given explicit support to the oft-reiterated Soviet view that the Court is not competent to interpret the Charter of the United Nations. None indicated dissent from the express rejection of this contention by the Court in the advisory opinion on Competence of the General Assembly for the Admission of a State to the United Nations.[33]

Although "impartiality" is a characteristic which is universally prized in a judicial tribunal, it must be kept in mind that the impartiality of a tribunal is always relative, never absolute. As already pointed out, in applying general standards to particular cases, courts unavoidably perform a law-developing function. They have to make decisions as to the direction in which the law is to be developed in its application to particular cases. Aside from the fact, already noted, that judges are human beings whose decisions cannot

31 ICJ Reports 1948, p. 15. The votes of these judges may have possibly been influenced by advance information that Albania and the United Kingdom had already concluded a special agreement providing for submission of the case regardless of the decision of the Court on the question of jurisdiction.

32 ICJ Reports 1949, pp. 4, 36, 37, 75, 113, 130, 244 and 250-51. In the advisory opinion on the International Status of South West Africa, ICJ Reports 1950, p. 128, the Polish judge joined the majority on all points while the Soviet and Yugoslav judges dissented in part.

33 ICJ Reports 1950, pp. 4 and 6; ICJ, Distr. 50/7. Cf. also *Conditions of Admission of a State to Membership in the United Nations (Article 4 of the Charter)*, ICJ Pleadings 1948, p. 29.

fail to be affected by their emotions, the "impartiality" of any tribunal is limited by the framework in which it operates. A court is an organ of the community, and its basic function is to serve the needs of the community. No standard of justice is so absolute that it can be expected to override the fundamental interests of the community or of its dominant members. Satisfaction of the desire to see justice done is usually one, but not the only one, of these interests. Law is a tool by which the community, led by its dominant member or group of members, seeks to achieve certain ends. It is the formalized expression of the long-range policy of the community. In the development of this policy not all members or groups of members of the community have equal influence. Law, therefore, is a policy designed to serve either the interests of the community as a whole or the interests of its dominant member or group of members. A court, in its decision-making capacity, is an organ for the administration of this policy. Its task is to make prevail the long-range policy of the community (even while developing and modifying it) over the conflicting interests of the particular members of the community and also over the conflicting short-range policies pursued by other organs of the community. So long as a court faithfully carries out this task, it is acting in accordance with law, and remains impartial even if its decisions in fact confer advantages on one part of the community at the expense of another. A judge ceases to be impartial if he lets himself be influenced by such considerations as his own personal advantage, personal liking or sympathy for a party to the case, or emotional preference for any relatively short-range policy not designed to effectuate the long-range policy he is called upon to implement. He is impartial if, undeterred by such considerations, he administers and develops the law in a way designed to accomplish its fundamental objectives, among which the preservation of the community is usually the supreme one.[34]

[34] *Fiat justitia, pereat mundus* is not a description of how courts usually behave. It is not the normal function of a court to be an instrument of the destruction or disruption of the community it serves by the application of

In the international community, which is much less well defined and organized than the modern national state, power is decentralized, and the long-range policy expressed in legal standards is consequently often vague, doubtful and unsupported by the determination of the most powerful members of the community to enforce it. International tribunals, whose powers and authority rest on the voluntary submission of states, may be justifiably cautious, in cases where the applicable standards of international law are not clear, in giving precedence to their own conceptions of what the long-range interests of the international community require over the interests of the particular parties to a dispute.[35]

The International Court, however, has shown an inclination, so far largely restricted to advisory opinions, to attach controlling weight to the requirements and interests of the international community as it sees them. Thus, as already noted, in the advisory opinion on Reparation for Injuries Suffered in the Service of the United Nations, it expressly referred to "the needs of the community" and the influence of "the requirements of international life" upon the development of international law.[36] Significantly, it said that "fifty states, representing the vast majority of the members of the international community, had the power, in conformity with international law, to bring into being an entity possessing objective international personality, not merely personality

---

standards of justice deemed to have absolute validity. It may be noted that in most systems of law the community itself, as organized in the state and represented by the government, is either not subject to the ordinary rules of law which control the relations of the members of the community or is at least accorded special privileges and exemptions. Anglo-American courts, for example, have developed and applied (except as otherwise directed by legislative enactments) the rules that the state cannot be sued without its consent, that prescription does not operate against the state, and that the state is not bound by the acts of its agents which are not actually authorized. These and other similar rules give the state a privileged position in relation to private persons.

35 This is also reflected in the fact that the standards administered and the procedure followed by international tribunals are generally subject to a greater degree of control by the parties than are the standards and procedures of judicial tribunals in modern states.

36 ICJ Reports 1949, p. 178. See above, p. 22.

recognized by them alone, together with capacity to bring international claims," and accordingly held, in the absence of precedent, that the United Nations had the capacity to bring international claims not only against its Members, but also against states which were not its Members. In effect, the Court adopted the view that the long-range policy of the international community, as shaped by the dominant group of its members (the United Nations), prevails, at least to some extent, over the interest of particular states in not having their international legal positions modified without their consent.[37] The Court evidently believed that in adopting this view it was not departing from the duty of impartiality. It is to be hoped that the Court will not exaggerate the actual role of the United Nations as the dominant policy-shaping element in the international community.[38]

The confidence reposed by the states in the Court is likely to be enhanced rather than diminished by a conservative approach on the part of the latter toward problems of its own jurisdiction and the development of international law. Too much eagerness to engage in judicial legislation may make states more reluctant to submit cases to the Court because of the uncertainty of outcome. The Court is also likely to win confidence by the cogency of the grounds given for its decisions and by the readiness with which it strives to give full effect, in the interpretation of treaties and other

---

37 ICJ Reports 1949, p. 185. See also the advisory opinion on the International Status of South West Africa, ICJ Reports 1950, pp. 128 and 136-38, where the Court held, on grounds which are formally rather tenuous, that the General Assembly of the United Nations had succeeded to the supervisory functions of the Council of the League of Nations with respect to the administration of mandated territories as a "sacred trust of civilization." The old Court had already shown a tendency to construe the powers of international organs broadly. See H. Lauterpacht, *The Development of International Law by the Permanent Court of International Justice*, pp. 48 and 72-78.

38 In this connection, it may be noted that at present the Court is composed exclusively of nationals of Members of the United Nations. In the old Court, at all times, at least one of the judges came from a state which was not a member of the League. It may be desirable to make the new Court more truly representative of the world community by the election of a judge from a non-member of the United Nations.

international instruments, to the discernible common design of the parties rather than to artificial rules of construction or general presumptions.[39]

The Bases of the Court's Jurisdiction

The jurisdiction of the Court over disputes submitted to it as contentious cases rests in principle on the consent of the parties. This consent can be given either (1) by a declaration recognizing as compulsory the jurisdiction of the Court, with or without limitation, under the "optional clause" of Article 36 of the Statute, or (2) by an undertaking in any other form to recognize as compulsory the jurisdiction of the Court with respect to a class of existing or future disputes, or (3) by an express or tacit agreement to submit a particular dispute to the Court.

As in the case of the Permanent Court "only states may be parties in cases before the Court" (Article 34 (1) of the new Statute). Neither individuals nor organizations other than states have standing before the Court, but public international organizations, at the request of the Court or on their own initiative, may present information relevant to cases before the Court.

Proposals to give the Court obligatory jurisdiction received strong support both at the time of the drafting of the original Statute in 1920 and at the time of drafting of the new Statute in 1945,[40] but were rejected on both occasions. Such proposals have been favored largely by the smaller powers. At the San Francisco Conference in 1945, a majority of the delegations favored obligatory jurisdiction, but the opposition of the Soviet Union and the United States led to the retention of the principle of jurisdiction based on the consent of

---

39 See, in this connection, Charles Cheney Hyde, *International Law Chiefly as Interpreted and Applied by the United States* (2nd revised ed., Boston, Little, Brown and Co., 1945), Vol. II, pp. 1486 ff., and H. Lauterpacht, "Restrictive Interpretation and the Principle of Effectiveness in the Interpretation of Treaties," *The British Year Book of International Law, 1949,* Vol. 26, p. 48.

40 See Manley O. Hudson, *op. cit.,* pp. 190-93.

the parties and of the "optional clause"[41] in Article 36, which, in its present form, reads as follows:

ARTICLE 36

1. The jurisdiction of the Court comprises all cases which the parties refer to it and all matters specially provided for in the Charter of the United Nations or in treaties and conventions in force.

2. The states parties to the present Statute may at any time declare that they recognize as compulsory *ipso facto* and without special agreement, in relation to any other state accepting the same obligation, the jurisdiction of the Court in all legal disputes concerning:

a. the interpretation of a treaty;

b. any question of international law;

c. the existence of any fact which, if established, would constitute a breach of an international obligation;

d. the nature or extent of the reparation to be made for the breach of an international obligation.

3. The declarations referred to above may be made unconditionally or on condition of reciprocity on the part of several or certain states, or for a certain time.

4. Such declarations shall be deposited with the Secretary-General of the United Nations, who shall transmit copies thereof to the parties to the Statute and to the Registrar of the Court.

5. Declarations made under Article 36 of the Statute of the Permanent Court of International Justice and which are still in force shall be deemed, as between the parties to the present Statute, to be acceptances of the compulsory jurisdiction of the International Court of Justice for the period which they still have to run and in accordance with their terms.

6. In the event of a dispute as to whether the Court has jurisdiction, the matter shall be settled by the decision of the Court.

---

41 See UNCIO *Documents,* Vol. XIII, pp. 390-92 and 557-59; Lawrence Preuss, "The International Court of Justice and the Problem of Compulsory Jurisdiction," Department of State *Bulletin,* Vol. XIII (1945), p. 471.

The reasons for the opposition of the Soviet and the United States delegations to obligatory jurisdiction merit some attention. As S. B. Krylov, one of the Soviet delegates at San Francisco and subsequently the Soviet member of the Court, tersely puts it, "the U.S.S.R. was guided by the necessity of defending the interests of the socialist state, the United States was apprehensive of opposition in the Senate to the ratification of the Charter and the Statute."[42] The Soviet position appears to derive from the Marxist theory that law is based on the will of the ruling classes. The interests and policies of the Soviet and the capitalist states are viewed as being so basically opposed that impartial adjudication of disputes of any importance between them is believed to be virtually impossible. M. Litvinov is reported to have declared at the Genoa Conference in 1922:

> Commander Hilton Young had asked whether it would be impossible to find a single impartial judge in the whole world. It was necessary to face the fact that there was not one world but two – a Soviet world and a non-Soviet world. Because there was no third world to arbitrate, he anticipated difficulties. . . . Only an angel could be unbiased in judging Russian affairs. . . .[43]

In a world still dominated by the capitalist states, the majority of the Court, according to this view, is bound to be composed of judges whose political sympathies would be on the side of capitalism and who would share the basic postulates on which the capitalist society is based. So long as the communist states remain in a minority, they cannot, in general, risk the submission of their differences with capitalist states to a body in which the rule of unanimity does not prevail.[44] The Soviet Union logically enough has not

---

42 S. B. Krylov, *Materialy k Istorii Organizatsii Ob'edinennykh Natsii* (Moscow, Izdatel'stvo Akademii Nauk SSSR, 1949), Vol. I, p. 212 n.

43 T. A. Taracouzio, *The Soviet Union and International Law* (New York, Macmillan Co., 1935), p. 296. See also Kathryn W. Davis, *The Soviets at Geneva* (Geneva, Librairie Kundig, 1934), pp. 221-22.

44 The Soviet doctrine is nowhere officially stated thus baldly, but see A. Y. Vyshinsky, "Mezhdunarodnoe Pravo i Mezhdunarodnaia Organizatsiia," *Sovetskoe Gosudarstvo i Pravo,* 1948, No. 1, p. 1; also his *Voprosy Mezhdu-*

accepted the compulsory jurisdiction of the Court under the "optional clause" and has often opposed the inclusion in treaties to which it is a signatory of provisions for the submission of disputes to the Court.

The fear of the United States delegation that a provision for the obligatory jurisdiction of the Court would encounter difficulties in the Senate was partly borne out in 1946 when the Senate attached reservations to the United States declaration of acceptance of the compulsory jurisdiction of the Court under the "optional clause." One of these reservations, sponsored by the Administration, excepted "disputes the solution of which the parties shall entrust to other tribunals by virtue of agreements already in existence or which may be concluded in the future." This reservation was similar to those made by many other states and has not aroused much comment.

More significant are the two reservations which respectively excepted "disputes with regard to matters which are essentially within the domestic jurisdiction of the United States of America as determined by the United States of America," and "disputes arising under a multilateral treaty, unless (1) all parties to the treaty affected by the decision are also parties to the case before the Court, or (2) the United States of America specifically agrees to jurisdiction."[45] These two reservations had been suggested by Mr. John Foster Dulles in a memorandum to the Senate Committee on Foreign Relations. Among the reasons advanced by Mr. Dulles for these reservations were that "it would be reckless to proceed precipitately," that the Court "has yet to win the confidence of the world community," and that "international law has not yet developed the scope and defi-

---

narodnogo Prava i Mezhdunarodnoi Politiki (Moscow, Gosudarstvennoe Izdatel'stvo Yuridicheskoi Literatury, 1949), p. 498 n. 69, and speeches in the United Nations General Assembly on 14 November and 17 November 1947, Official Records of the Second Session of the General Assembly, Plenary Meetings, 16 September-29 November 1947, Vol. II, pp. 877-86 and 1047-53. Cf. *Memorandum on the Soviet Doctrine and Practice with Respect to Arbitral Procedure,* United Nations Doc. A/CN.4/36, 21 November 1950.

45 Department of State *Bulletin,* Vol. XV (1946), p. 452.

niteness necessary to permit international disputes generally to be resolved by judicial rather than political tests."[46] The domestic jurisdiction reservation was introduced by Senator Connally and approved by 51 to 12 votes; the multilateral treaty reservation was introduced by Senator Vandenberg and accepted without objection. Debate in the Senate revealed that there was apprehension that without the domestic jurisdiction reservation the Court might invade such fields as immigration, the tariff and the control of the Panama Canal. The effect of this reservation is to leave the United States legally free to refuse to submit any dispute to the Court, although for moral and political reasons this freedom is not likely to be exercised unreasonably. It may be also noted that all these reservations operate reciprocally.[47]

A total of forty-five states were at one time or another bound by declarations recognizing the compulsory jurisdiction of the Permanent Court of International Justice under the "optional clause." As of 1 February 1951, thirty-five states had accepted the compulsory jurisdiction of the new Court.[48] Although the Statute is largely silent on the matter, it has been the practice of many states to make their acceptance of the Court's jurisdiction under the "optional clause" sub-

---

46 Mr. Dulles further proposed to except "disputes where the law necessary for decision is not found in existing treaties and conventions to which the United States is a party and where there has not been prior agreement by the United States as to the applicable principles of international law." U. S. Congress, Senate Committee on Foreign Relations, *Compulsory Jurisdiction, International Court of Justice,* Hearings . . . on Senate Res. 196 . . ., 11, 12 and 15 July 1946, pp. 43-45. This proposal failed of adoption in the Senate.

47 On the American reservations see Lawrence Preuss, "The International Court of Justice, the Senate, and Matters of Domestic Jurisdiction," *American Journal of International Law,* Vol. 40 (1946), p. 720, and documents there cited; Francis O. Wilcox, "The United States Accepts Compulsory Jurisdiction," *ibid.,* p. 699; Quincy Wright, "The International Court of Justice and the Interpretation of Multilateral Treates," *American Journal of International Law,* Vol. 41 (1947), p. 445. See also Ernest A. Gross, "Impact of the United Nations Upon Domestic Jurisdiction," Department of State *Bulletin,* Vol. XVIII (1948), p. 259. Domestic jurisdiction reservations in forms similar to that adopted by the United States have since been made by France, Mexico and Pakistan.

48 Including seventeen states who were bound by virtue of their declarations under the old Statute and Article 36 (5) of the new Statute.

ject to far-reaching reservations of various types. Very frequent is the limitation of the acceptance to future disputes or disputes arising "with regard to situations or facts subsequent" to the date of acceptance. Some states have excepted certain classes of controversies, as for instance "pecuniary claims" (El Salvador) or those relating to "territorial status" (Iran). Guatemala's declaration "does not cover the dispute between England and Guatemala concerning the restoration of the territory of Belize, which the government of Guatemala would, as it has proposed, agree to submit to the judgment of the Court, if the case were decided *ex aequo et bono*. . . ."[49]

Many of the declarations are valid only for a term of years, others are of indefinite duration. Declarations containing a minimum of significant limitations have been made by Bolivia, Brazil, China, Denmark, Dominican Republic, Haiti, Honduras, Liechtenstein, Nicaragua, Norway, Panama, Paraguay, the Philippines, Switzerland, Thailand and Uruguay.[50]

During the existence of the Permanent Court of International Justice eleven contentious proceedings were instituted by unilateral applications relying on the "optional clause." In two of the cases the Court held that it lacked jurisdiction, in five the proceedings were discontinued before the Court considered the basis of its jurdisdiction, and in one reliance on the "optional clause" was withdrawn. In three cases the Court exercised jurisdiction in whole or in

---

49 This was not acceptable to the United Kingdom. However, it has expressly accepted the jurisdiction of the Court "in all legal disputes concerning the interpretation, application or validity of any treaty relating to the boundaries of British Honduras, and over any questions arising out of any conclusion which the Court may reach with regard to such treaty." See "The Belize Controversy Between Great Britain and Guatemala," *The British Year Book of International Law 1947*, Vol. 24, p. 406.

50 For the contents of the declarations, see Yearbooks of ICJ; see also U. S. Department of State, *Compulsory Jurisdiction of the International Court of Justice*, Publication 3540 (1949). For analyses of the declarations, see Manley O. Hudson, *op. cit.*, pp. 465-73; Edvard Hambro, "Some Observations of the Compulsory Jurisdiction of the International Court of Justice," *The British Year Book of International Law 1948*, Vol. 25, p. 133,

part on the basis of the clause.[51] In the new Court, proceedings have been begun in two cases in reliance on the clause.

The large number of reservations attached to the acceptances of the compulsory jurisdiction of the Court under the "optional clause" and the fact that such reservations operate reciprocally have undoubtedly reduced the practical usefulness of the clause. Attempts have been made to extend the jurisdiction of the Court by provisions in general or regional treaties for pacific settlement, including the unratified "Geneva Protocol,"[52] the General Act for the Pacific Settlement of Disputes (1928, revised in 1949), and the Inter-American Pact of Bogotá (1948).[53] As of 1 February 1951, only a limited number of states, most of which had accepted compulsory jurisdiction of the Court under the "optional clause," were bound by these treaties (which do not exclude the possibility of making far-reaching reservations) and there has been apparently no attempt to rely upon them in any proceeding before the Court. Similar provisions have also been inserted in numerous bilateral treaties dealing with the settlement of disputes, and have served as the basis of the Court's jurisdiction in at least two cases.[54]

It has become common practice to include provisions for submission of disputes to the Court in multilateral and bilateral treaties dealing with particular subjects. Before the second World War, for example, such provisions appeared in the constitution of the International Labour Organisation, international instruments for the protection of minorities, League of Nations mandates, and conventions on transit and communications; they served as the basis for the Court's jurisdiction in a number of cases.[55] Since the war provisions

---

51 See Manley O. Hudson, *op. cit.*, p. 481.

52 See David Hunter Miller, *The Geneva Protocol* (New York, Macmillan Co., 1925), and *International Conciliation,* No. 205, December, 1924 (New York, Carnegie Endowment for International Peace, 1924).

53 The relevant texts are collected, with notes, in U. S. Department of State, *Compulsory Jurisdiction of the International Court of Justice, op. cit.*, pp. 19-21.

54 Manley O. Hudson, *op. cit.*, pp. 443-45.

55 *Ibid.*, pp. 438-43. Article 37 of the new Statute provides: "Whenever a treaty or convention in force provides for reference of a matter to a tribunal

of this type have also appeared in a large number of multilateral and bilateral instruments. They are found in the constitutions of several specialized agencies, trusteeship agreements, and multilateral conventions concluded under the auspices of the United Nations. Recent commercial treaties between the United States and other nations have contained clauses for the submission of disputes to the Court.[56]

In the absence of an applicable general provision by which a state has accepted the jurisdiction of the Court, consent to proceedings before the tribunal may be given expressly either in the form of a special agreement or otherwise, or tacitly, as by failing to object to the institution of a proceeding and appearing to answer on the merits, or by intervening in a proceeding.[57]

Codification and Acceptance of the Court's Jurisdiction

Among the reasons given for the failure of some states to accept unconditionally the jurisdiction of the Court is the uncertainty of international law. Codification is said to be necessary to eliminate this obstacle.[58] There can be no doubt that international law is in some respects vague and uncer-

---

to have been instituted by the League of Nations, or to the Permanent Court of International Justice, the matter shall, as between the parties to the present Statute, be referred to the International Court of Justice."

56 See, *e.g.*, Article 28 of the 1946 treaty with China, *Treaties and Other International Acts Series* 1871. Relevant passages from the various instruments providing for the jurisdiction of the Court are regularly published in the Yearbooks of the Court.

57 Manley O. Hudson, *op. cit.*, pp. 410-11, 416-24, 435-38; Edvard Hambro, *op. cit.*, pp. 153-55.

58 The Charter of the United Nations, in Article 13 (1a), directs the General Assembly to "initiate studies and make recommendations for the purpose of . . . encouraging the progressive development of international law and its codification." Pursuant to this provision, an International Law Commission composed of experts has been appointed by the General Assembly and is engaged in the study of several topics. For recent discussions of the problem of codification of international law, see Green H. Hackworth, "The International Court of Justice and the Codification of International Law," *American Bar Association Journal,* Vol. 32 (1946), p. 81; Sir Cecil Hurst, "A Plea for the Codification of International Law on New Lines," The Grotius Society, *Transactions for the Year 1946,* Vol. 32, p. 135; R. Y. Jennings, "The Progressive Development of International Law and Its Codification," *British Year Book of International Law 1947,* Vol. 24, p. 301.

tain, and that as a result some governments are reluctant to expose themselves to the danger of a judgment by the Court adverse to a legal position they have consistently maintained. Codification may eventually help to reduce the uncertainty of international law, but recent experience indicates that efforts at codification are not likely to be very successful in the near future. Although certain of the rules of war and neutrality were codified at the Hague Conferences of 1899 and 1907 with some measure of success, the Codification Conference which met at The Hague in 1930 under the auspices of the League of Nations and which tackled three of the most controversial topics in the law of peace (nationality, responsibility of states for injuries to aliens, and territorial waters) was an almost complete failure. At such conferences, the various delegations usually attempt to insert in the proposed conventions the views favored by their respective governments even if they know that such views are contrary to the established practice, and the result is either outright disagreement (which increases rather than reduces the uncertainty of international law) or vaguely worded compromises which do little to clear up controversial points. Even the Hague Conventions on the rules of war and neutrality leave many questions unanswered.

Furthermore, express statement of a rule in a convention which is ratified by some but not all states may have the result of weakening the authority of the rule as part of customary law by placing its general acceptance in doubt.

The experience of modern states indicates, moreover, that codification does not prevent new problems from constantly arising and being taken care of by some form of judicial legislation. For example, in France, a country in which the law is said to be completely codified and in which the judges are not supposed to lay down general principles in their opinions, the rules of liability for injuries caused by negligence have been in fact developed almost entirely by judicial decisions on the basis of three short articles (1382, 1383 and 1384) of the *Code Civile*. Codification thus does not preclude the need for the interpretation and development of the law by the courts and does not assure its certainty.

Since the Court itself may be instrumental in the development of international law by its decisions, reluctance to accept the jurisdiction of the Court leads to a vicious circle. Disputes are not submitted to the Court because the law is uncertain; but the law remains uncertain partly because the Court has no opportunity to refine and develop it. The leading states of the world whose announced goal is the creation and maintenance of the rule of law in international affairs must decide whether this goal is worth the risks of unconditional submission to the jurisdiction of the Court, even if the law administered by the Court is still in many respects unsettled. It is important to make a start in the right direction. The Supreme Court of the United States has decided many cases between the states of the Union although it had no body of rules more definite than those of international law — and sometimes not even those — to apply in such cases. Early in its history, the Supreme Court rejected objections to its jurisdiction based on the absence of a definite body of law applicable to interstate controversies, and its eminent historian, Charles Warren, has pointed out that

> thus far . . . the Supreme Court has never met with any form of controversy, or any condition productive of conflict between the States of the Union, for which the Court has been unable to discover a formula for its solution by resort to some principle of law, international or otherwise, appropriate to afford just treatment to States entitled to an equality of right. If no actual precedent has existed, the Court has always found it possible to settle the case by equitable consideration of the needs and relations of human societies, and by logical extension of general principles of justice derived from established international, common, or civil law.[59]

It is of interest that while a great power, the United Kingdom, has offered on several occasions to refer its disputes to

59 "The Supreme Court and Disputes Between States," *International Conciliation,* No. 366, January, 1941, pp. 39-40.

the Court, some of the smaller powers have shown themselves disinclined to have their claims adjudicated on the basis of law. Argentina and Chile, for example, have declined a British offer to refer to the Court conflicting territorial claims in the Antarctic.[60]

Factors Limiting the Court's Role

The fundamental limitation on the usefulness of the Court as an organ for the settlement of international disputes is the fact that not all conflicts of interest are capable of being terminated by judicial techniques within the existing legal framework. It is possible to argue that theoretically all disputes, of whatever origin, can be settled by judicial techniques, either by the application of existing law or through the creation of new legal standards or by giving the tribunal the power to decide *ex aequo et bono* without regard to legal standards; in practice, such a result has never been achieved in any community.[61]

Even in the best organized states, many conflicts of interest cannot be terminated by judicial proceedings. If, for instance, a group of workers makes a demand upon the employers for higher wages, and the demand is turned down, the workers may attempt to sue the employers in a court of law; but if there is no legal standard entitling the plaintiffs to the wages they are demanding, the court will dismiss the case on the ground that the employers are under no duty

---

60 Guatemala's attitude has already been mentioned. It is hardly surprising, in view of the Soviet attitude toward the Court, that the USSR and its friends rejected in 1948 a British proposal to have the Court pass on the rights of the United Kingdom under the treaties relating to the Danube.

61 The literature on the problem of "justiciability" of international disputes is voluminous; for some representative discussions, see H. Lauterpacht, *The Function of Law in the International Community*; Edward Hallett Carr, *The Twenty Years' Crisis 1919-1939* (2nd ed., London, Macmillan Co., 1946), ch. 12; Hans Kelsen, *Peace Through Law* (Chapel Hill, University of North Carolina Press, 1944); Hans Kelsen, "Compulsory Adjudication of International Disputes," *American Journal of International Law*, Vol. 37 (1943), p. 397; Louis B. Sohn, "Exclusion of Political Disputes from Judicial Settlement," *American Journal of International Law*, Vol. 38 (1944), p. 694; Grant Gilmore, "The International Court of Justice," *Yale Law Journal*, Vol. 55 (1946), pp. 1060-64.

to grant the demand. Legally, the controversy may now be regarded as closed and the dispute "settled"; experience indicates, however, that the workers may refuse to regard the conflict as terminated and use economic and other means at their disposal, such as strikes, "slow-downs" or even violence to induce the employers to grant their demands. The state may declare illegal and endeavor to suppress resort to such means, but the workers may still attempt to resolve the conflict in their favor either by using their political strength to change the law peaceably or by staging a revolution. It is not helpful to pretend that all disputes of this nature can be actually terminated by decisions of judicial tribunals. Even if the law were changed so as to provide for some standards of "fair wages" to be applied in all wage disputes by courts or arbitral tribunals, or for compulsory arbitration of such disputes *ex aequo et bono,* there would still remain the possibility of dissatisfaction with the prescribed standards or with the results of the work of the tribunals; and if the dissatisfaction were strong enough, political action, peaceful or violent, might again be resorted to. The extent to which conflicts of interest are resolved by judicial or quasi-judicial proceedings varies among the different communities and does not remain constant; there always remain some areas of interest, however, in which conflicts are settled only by the matching of economic and political strength. The spectre of revolution is at times indistinct, but it is never completely exorcised.

A few illustrations may be useful in showing how this principle operates in the international arena. Austria and Germany bowed in 1931 to the contention of France and her allies, supported by an advisory opinion of the Court, that their proposed customs union would be contrary to the international obligations of Austria, and called it off. Agitation for union between the two countries continued, however, and culminated in the annexation of Austria by Hitler in 1938, when the political and economic balance of power had shifted in Germany's favor. Similarly, an advisory opinion of the Court supported in 1931 the contention of Lithuania that she was under no legal duty to reopen railroad traffic with Poland,[62] but the absence of communications between the two neighbors could hardly be regarded as a satisfactory situation, and in 1938 Lithuania yielded to a virtual ultimatum of Poland demanding the establishment of more normal relations. It is evident that in neither case did judicial proceedings before the Court suffice to dispose of the conflict.

It is clear that a controversy as to how a discretionary power should be exercised cannot be resolved by the application of legal standards but calls for a political settlement.

In international relations the inadequacy of the judicial settlement of disputes is enhanced by the weakness of international law and by the absence of organized enforcement of the law by superior power. There is, moreover, no orderly and effective procedure for changing the law by peaceful methods. As a result, in the international community the areas of interest in which conflicts are resolved by judicial proceedings are relatively small. Resort to violence is less likely to be unprofitable than it is in well-organized modern states. In recent times rapid shifts in the balance of power have aggravated the situation.

It is significant that the application of legal standards to international conflicts of interest was more frequent and, temporarily, more successful during the early period of the life of the League of Nations, when the states which created and led the League were in a favorable power position, than during the later period when the balance of power was rapidly shifting in favor of the states dissatisfied with the *status quo*. Yet the power behind the law is never merely physical; it always rests on the determination of individuals and groups of individuals to lend their strength to the support of the law. Rational appreciation of the advantages of peaceful and orderly settlement of disputes on the basis of

---

62 PCIJ, *Publications,* Series A/B, No. 42.

ascertainable standards and the more emotional but perhaps no less efficacious attachment to the principles of fairness, moral obligation and good faith, may combine to make possible the extention of the area within which the application of judicial techniques to conflicts of interest is fruitful. The decision of a government to have or not to have its dispute with another government adjudicated by a judicial tribunal is usually based on a balancing of the risk of losing out in such a proceeding, where the power factor has relatively little effect, against the recognizable rational advantages and emotional satisfactions of participation in it. The greater the interest at stake, the less likelihood there is of a contestant foregoing the advantages of a political settlement in which the power factor would work in his favor.

In some cases, reluctance to submit a dispute to a settlement by either judicial or political procedures may be based on a calculation that the passage of time will improve the power position of the contestant, or on the feeling that there is no advantage in having the dispute settled at all (its continuance may, for instance, serve a useful domestic political purpose) ; or a government may be convinced that its interests will be best served by the application of the vaguer standards of fairness and justice than of those of law, in which case it may insist on the submission of the dispute to a judicial tribunal to be decided *ex aequo et bono.*

All international disputes have both legal and political elements in varying proportions. The question whether a dispute is "legal" is a relative one, and the answer depends on the view taken by the contestants. If they all feel that the dispute can be effectively terminated by the application of legal standards, it is "legal," but if at least one of them does not share this attitude, the dispute must be regarded as primarily "political." This criterion also determines whether a "question" which has given rise to an international controversy is or is not "legal."

Problem of Enforcement of the Court's Decisions

An important limitation upon a tribunal's usefulness is the possible failure of its decisions to command obedience. A judgment of the Court is final and without appeal and compliance with the decisions of the Court in contentious cases is legally obligatory upon the parties to such cases, but there is no enforcement machinery. The Court has no marshals or sheriffs at its disposal. In case of non-compliance with a judgment, the Security Council "may, if it deems necessary, make recommendations or decide upon measures to be taken to give effect to the judgment."[63] It is not under a duty to do so. No occasion has in fact arisen in which either the League Council or the Security Council has been asked to enforce a judgment of the Court.

May a state use force to compel compliance with a judgment in its favor? Article 2 of the Charter provides in part:

> 4. All Members shall refrain in their international relations from the threat or use of force against the territorial integrity or political independence of any state, or in any other manner inconsistent with the Purposes of the United Nations.

Is the threat or use of force to compel compliance with the decisions of the Court inconsistent with this and the other provisions for peaceful settlement contained in Article 1 (1) and Article 2 (3)? If so, would a supporting resolution of the General Assembly suffice to remove the inconsistency? To what extent do these provisions affect the

---

[63] United Nations Charter, Article 94 (2). The Covenant of the League provided in Article 13 (4) that in "the event of any failure to carry out such an award or decision, the Council shall propose what steps should be taken to give effect thereto." On the interpretation of these provisions see Leland M. Goodrich and Edvard Hambro, *Charter of the United Nations: Commentary and Documents* (Revised ed., Boston, World Peace Foundation, 1949), pp. 485-87; Hans Kelsen, *The Law of the United Nations,* pp. 539-44, 720-21; F. Blaine Sloan, "Enforcement of Arbitral Awards in International Agencies," *The Arbitration Journal,* New Series, Vol. III (1948), pp. 140-46; Edvard Hambro, *L'Exécution des Sentences Internationales* (Liège, H. Vaillant-Carmanne, 1936), pp. 68-95; Constantin Vulcan, "L'Exécution des Décisions de la Cour Internationale de Justice d'après la Charte des Nations Unies," *Revue Générale de Droit International Public,* Vol. 51 (1947), p. 187.

legal position of states not members of the United Nations? Is there a rule of general international law, as distinguished from the Charter, limiting the freedom of states to use force to maintain their rights under international law as determined by the Court? In the absence of practice or clear consensus, no definite answers to these questions are ventured here.

If self-help in the enforcement of the Court's judgments is deemed to be forbidden by the Charter or by recently developed principles of general international law, the evident effect is the weakening of the rule of law in the international community, since the Security Council is not specifically directed by the Charter to enforce such judgments. This is hardly in consonance with the underlying purposes of the movement toward the consolidation of the international community into a stronger organization.[64]

Article 51 of the Charter could on occasion serve to justify the use of force to carry out a judgment of the Court. For example, the forcible occupation of a territory by the state entitled to its possession under a judgment of the Court might be regarded as a lawful exercise of authority, armed resistance to which by another state would constitute an "armed attack" within the meaning of Article 51.

Settlement Through Contentious Proceedings

Most of the disputes handled by the Court in contentious cases were not such as to threaten the peace at the time they arose. They involved such questions as the passage of a French steamer carrying munitions to Poland through the Kiel Canal, the treatment of a Greek concessionaire in Palestine by the British mandatory administration, the powers of

---

[64] "Rien ne peut être plus dangereux pour la communauté internationale que les sentences qui restent lettre morte." Edvard Hambro, *op. cit.*, p. 70. It may be maintained that the prohibition of resort to war "as an instrument of national policy" contained in the Pact of Paris is not necessarily inconsistent with the use of force to compel compliance with international law, since the observance of international law must be regarded as a policy of the whole international community and not primarily as "national policy." Cf. *ibid.*, pp. 115-27. See, in general, Constantin Vulcan, *op. cit.*

an arbitrator between Bulgaria and Greece under the treaty of peace, the expropriation of certain German-owned properties in Polish Upper Silesia, the exercise of criminal jurisdiction by Turkey over a French merchant marine officer after a collision between a French and a Turkish vessel, the position of German minority schools in Polish Upper Silesia, the mode of payment of Serbian and Brazilian loans issued in France, the maintenance of certain "free zones" on the French-Swiss border, the jurisdiction of the International Commission of the Oder, the right of the Governor of Memel to dismiss the President of the Directorate of the same territory, sovereignty in Eastern Greenland, the restitution by Czechoslovakia of lands belonging to a Hungarian university, the rights of a French firm arising out of a concession for lighthouses in Greek territory, the position of a British river transport operator in the Belgian Congo, the effect of Czechoslovak land reforms on Hungarian landowners, diversion of water from the Meuse, the seizure in Lithuania of a railroad claimed by an Estonian company, the treatment of certain Belgian companies in Bulgaria and Greece, and the granting of diplomatic asylum to a Peruvian political leader in the Colombian Embassy in Lima.[65]

A few of these disputes, such as that between Denmark and Norway over sovereignty in Eastern Greenland, concerned matters of potentially great importance to the states concerned. Nevertheless, the very fact of submission of these disputes to the Court generally indicated willingness on the part of the contestants to seek and abide by a settlement arrived at by judicial techniques within the framework of existing law rather than by procedures in which power-political pressures could be used.[66] It is not surprising,

[65] The contentious cases pending on 1 February 1951 involved a further question arising out of the diplomatic asylum granted by the Colombian Embassy in Lima, the location of the base line from which Norwegian territorial waters may be measured, and the commercial treaty rights of the United States in French Morocco.

[66] In some cases, the determination of the legal position of the parties was preliminary to a more comprehensive settlement of the dispute by agreement. This was true, for instance, in the matter of payment of Serbian loans issued in France.

therefore, that the judgments of the Court have been in principle obeyed in all these cases.[67]

The Court's judgments have been occasionally criticized as vague or inconclusive, but an examination of the record often shows that the inconclusive character of a judgment is due to the failure of the parties to submit appropriate questions.[68]

The Corfu Channel Case

Only one case before the Court has been directly related to the use of armed force between the parties. This was the Corfu Channel case. The British government first demanded from Albania an apology and compensation. The Albanian reply was considered unsatisfactory by the United Kingdom, which then complained to the Security Council, seeking to place responsibility for the incident on Albania and asserting that the laying of a clandestine minefield was in violation of a Hague Convention and "a crime against humanity." The Albanian government was invited to participate in the proceedings in the Security Council without a vote on the condition that it accept for the purposes of the case all the obligations of a Member of the United Nations. The invitation was accepted by Albania. Following an examination of the evidence presented to the Security Council and a report by a sub-committee on the facts of the case, the Council voted 7 to 2, with one abstention (the United Kingdom, as a party to the dispute, not taking part in the voting), to find that an unnotified minefield had been laid in the Corfu

67 In a few cases, practical difficulties were encountered in making the payments pursuant to judgments. See Manley O. Hudson, *op. cit.*, p. 596. Many of the decisions of the Court have not required the payment of money.

68 See, *e.g.*, *The New York Times*, 21 November 1950, for a criticism of the judgment in the case which arose out of the granting of diplomatic asylum in the Colombian Embassy in Lima to Victor R. Haya de la Torre, a Peruvian political leader, as inconclusive since it failed to indicate whether Colombia was under a duty to surrender the fugitive to Peru; an examination of the submissions of the parties shows that the question of surrender was not before the Court. ICJ Reports 1950, pp. 266 and 402. This question was subsequently submitted to the Court by Colombia in a separate application.

Channel with the knowledge of the Albanian government. Since the Soviet Union voted against the resolution, it did not pass. The representative of the United Kingdom subsequently proposed that the Security Council recommend "that the United Kingdom and the Albanian Governments should immediately refer the dispute to the International Court of Justice in accordance with the provisions of the Statute of the Court." This proposal was adopted by 8 to 0 votes, with two abstentions (the USSR and Poland).[69]

The proceedings in the Court were begun by an application filed by the United Kingdom. Albania raised objections to the jurisdiction of the Court, but was held to have submitted to it by a letter dated 2 July 1947, addressed to the Deputy-Registrar of the Court.[70] The United Kingdom also advanced, as an alternative basis for the jurisdiction of the Court, the contention that Albania was bound by the recommendation of the Security Council to submit the dispute to the tribunal. This contention was based on the view that the recommendations of the Security Council under Article 36 of the Charter have obligatory force,[71] and the fact that Albania had accepted all the obligations of a member of the United Nations for the purpose of the case. The Court found it unnecessary to pass on this contention, but eight of the judges, including seven of the regular members of the Court, took pains to reject it expressly in separate opinions.[72]

---

69 For a summary of the proceedings in the Security Council, see the *Yearbook of the United Nations, 1946-1947,* pp. 392-94.

70 Judgment of March 25th, 1948, ICJ Reports 1948, p. 15. The Soviet, Polish and Yugoslav judges joined in this holding, while the judge *ad hoc* appointed by Albania dissented. Immediately after the delivery of this judgment, the Court was notified of a special agreement between the parties formulating the questions submitted to the Court. Albania later challenged the jurisdiction of the Court to fix the amount of compensation due the United Kingdom, but the objection was overruled by the Court. ICJ Reports 1949, p. 4.

71 The relevant provisions of the Charter are Articles 36 and 25. Reference was also made to Article 24 (2).

72 ICJ Reports 1948, pp. 31 and 33. Many of the unofficial commentators on the Charter seem to agree that Article 36 of the Charter does not constitute an additional basis for the jurisdication of the Court. See, *e.g.,* Leland M. Goodrich and Edvard Hambro, *op. cit.,* pp. 254-58; Hans Kelsen, *op. cit.,*

After the Corfu Channel dispute reached the Court, it was disposed of quietly, in a judicial atmosphere, and gave no further trouble to the international community. It appears to have been eminently a case for judicial, rather than political, settlement; the questions involved were those of facts and of law; there was no necessity for political adjustments. The Court's investigation of the facts with the assistance of experts was much more thorough than that attempted by the sub-committee of the Security Council. Albania cooperated in this investigation, as, for instance, by admitting the experts to Albanian territory. Later, however, it refused to recognize the jurisdiction of the Court to fix the amount of compensation due to the United Kingdom and has declined to pay the amount awarded,[73] thus becoming the first state in history to refuse in principle to comply with a decision of the Court in a contentious proceeding to which it was a party. Nevertheless, the judgment of the Court was calmly received by the parties[74] and the British government made no request to the Security Council to help it collect the award.

No "veto" obstructed the majority in making a decision. The Court's judgment, as noted in the preceding chapter, also provides guidance for the future with respect to the passage of foreign warships through territorial waters in international straits. A political decision by the Security Council would have had much less weight as a precedent and would have probably enjoyed no greater respect as a judgment. It is to be regretted that the United Kingdom did not at the very beginning offer to refer the dispute to the Court, as it should have done under Article 33 of the Charter, instead of carrying it directly before the Security Council. In

---

pp. 444-50 and 517; Eduardo Jiménez de Aréchaga, *Voting and the Handling of Disputes in the Security Council,* United Nations Studies, No. 5, (New York, Carnegie Endowment for International Peace, 1950), pp. 110-11. There would seem to be nothing in the Charter, however, to prevent the Security Council from finding that the failure of a state to submit a dispute to the Court in accordance with a recommendation under Article 36 of the Charter is a threat to the peace, and from taking enforcement action under Chapter VII to remove this threat.

73 ICJ Reports 1949, p. 244.

74 *Ibid.,* p. 4.

this case the Soviet veto, by preventing the passage of a resolution condemnatory of Albania in the Security Council and thus inducing the Council to recommend the submission of the dispute to the Court, apparently saved the United Nations from a blunder and played a constructive role.

Use of the Court By States

It is regrettable that no offer to submit to the Court the dispute between the United States and Yugoslavia growing out of the shooting down of two United States military aircraft in 1946 was made by either party;[75] and that no such offer was made in connection with the dispute between the United States and the Soviet Union concerning the disappearance in the spring of 1950 of a United States military aircraft after an encounter with Soviet aircraft over or near the Baltic Sea. Both incidents involved issues of fact and points of law more suitable for judicial than political determination.

The Corfu Channel case was the only dispute submitted by the parties to the new Court prior to 1949. There was some apprehension at the apparent reluctance of states to use the Court, and in 1947 two draft resolutions were introduced in the Sixth Committee of the General Assembly of the United Nations on the desirability of using the tribunal. The ensuing discussion "revealed a very general feeling of regret and concern at the indifference too often shown for the legal aspects of matters and at the disregard shown in recent years for arbitral and judicial methods."[76] On 14 November 1947, the General Assembly adopted a resolution in the following terms:

The General Assembly,

Considering that, in virtue of Article 1 of the Charter, international disputes should be settled in conformity with the principles of justice and international law;

---

75 The United States threatened to report to the Security Council but did not mention the Court. See note of 21 August 1946, Department of State *Bulletin,* Vol. XV (1946), pp. 417-18.

76 ICJ *Yearbook 1947-1948,* p. 16.

Considering that the International Court of Justice could settle or assist in settling such disputes if, by the full application of the provisions of the Charter and of the Statute of the Court, more frequent use were made of its services:

1. *Draws the attention* of the States which have not yet accepted the compulsory jurisdiction of the Court in accordance with Article 36, paragraphs 2 and 5, of the Statute, to the desirability of the greatest possible number of States accepting this jurisdiction with as few reservations as possible;

2. *Draws the attention* of States Members to the advantage of inserting in conventions and treaties arbitration clauses providing, without prejudice to Article 95 of the Charter, for the submission of disputes which may arise from the interpretation or application of such conventions or treaties, preferably and as far as possible to the International Court of Justice;

3. *Recommends* as a general rule that States should submit their legal disputes to the International Court of Justice.[77]

In 1949 and 1950 five contentious cases were submitted by states to the Court; one was later withdrawn.

The possibility of resort to the Court has probably induced the settlement of many disputes by direct negotiations. This, of course, is most likely to happen if there is a treaty obligation to accept the jurisdiction of the Court. Ake Hammarskjöld, the Registrar of the Court from 1922 to 1936, has stated that to his knowledge dozens of disputes were settled by negotiation after the parties had been faced with the possibility of resort to the Court.[78] Clarification of the issues resulting from the preparation of a case for trial before the Court may also account for settlements by direct agreement after the proceedings had begun.

---

[77] Official Records of the Second Session of the General Assembly, Resolutions, 16 September-29 November 1947, United Nations Doc. A/519, pp. 103-04; also ICJ *Yearbook 1947-1948*, p. 20. See also Yuen-li Liang, "Notes on Legal Questions Concerning the United Nations," *American Journal of International Law*, Vol. 42 (1948), pp. 439-44. The resolution was adopted by 45 to 6 votes with 3 abstentions. The opposition came from the Soviet bloc.

[78] A Hammarskjöld, *Juridiction Internationale* (Leiden, A. W. Sijthoff, 1938), pp. 76 and 391-92.

The political organs of the United Nations cannot normally compel states to submit their disputes to the Court as contentious cases, but Article 36 (3) of the Charter lays down the policy that in making recommendations for the settlement of disputes "the Security Council should also take into consideration that legal disputes should as a general rule be referred by the parties to the International Court of Justice," and this policy would seem to be equally applicable to recommendations made by the General Assembly. From the point of view of those seeking to preserve peace, the advantages of having a dispute taken from a political to a judicial body, where proceedings are not televised, there is no compulsive logorrhea, arguments are made calmly, and decisions are taken by simple majorities of judges removed from direct political pressures, would seem to be considerable. But, as already indicated, not all conflicts can be resolved by the legal method. The Corfu Channel case is the only dispute a political organ of the United Nations has recommended for submission to the Court.

The Permanent Court of International Justice, although it was open to states in all parts of the world, and although it had several members from the Western Hemisphere and from the Far East, dealt almost exclusively with disputes which arose in Europe and the adjoining areas of the Mediterranean and the Middle East.[79] The new Court has already handled one case between two Latin American states and has before it a dispute between France and the United States. It is truly a tribunal with world-wide functions, and its further development as such would be symbolic of the essential unity of mankind and responsive to the need for foster-

[79] The only cases involving substantial interests of states located outside of the region of Europe were those of the Brazilian loans issued in France (PCIJ, *Publications,* Series A, Nos. 20/21) and of the denunciation of the treaty between Belgium and China (proceedings terminated at the request of Belgium, the plaintiff state, PCIJ, *Publications,* Series A, Nos. 18/19). Japan appeared nominally as one of the Principal Allied and Associated Powers in two of the cases arising from the peace settlement in Europe. The Oscar Chinn case (PCIJ, *Publications,* Series A/B, No. 63) involved the interests of Belgium and Great Britain in Central Africa.

ing the uniformity of international law and the growth of a world community spirit. If the pressure of work eventually necessitates the establishment of additional tribunals, the Court should retain a world-wide appellate jurisdiction.[80]

The Function of Advisory Opinions

The function of advisory proceedings before the Court in the settlement of disputes has been somewhat different from that of proceedings in contentious cases. The very fact that a request for an advisory opinion on a question directly connected with a dispute between states is made by an international political organ is usually an indication that the states concerned have not agreed to settle the dispute by a binding judicial decision within the framework of existing law. There is, of course, nothing to prevent two or more states from agreeing to consider an advisory opinion as binding upon them and as a definitive settlement of the dispute, but the same result can be accomplished more directly by the submission of the dispute as a contentious case. It is not surprising, therefore, that there have been very few cases in which states agreed in advance to give definite legal effect to an advisory opinion, and that in several cases the interested states expressly declared, either in advance or subsequently, that they did not regard themselves bound by such an opinion.[81]

---

[80] The decision of the Court in the Colombian-Peruvian asylum case (ICJ Reports 1950, p. 266), in which it refused to recognize the existence of a general or regional rule of international law permitting the granting of diplomatic asylum to persons wanted for trial as political offenders, was criticized by Colombian spokesmen as having been made mainly by European judges unfamiliar with Latin American conditions and as impairing the usefulness of the Court for Latin American states. *The New York Times,* 20 November and 21 November 1950. It must be noted, however, that the five Latin American judges (including two judges *ad hoc*) who participated in the decision split among themselves in varying proportions on the several issues in the case, that only seven of the sixteen judges who sat in the case were from Europe, and that Colombia subsequently submitted an additional question to the Court (1950, General List No. 14, Application Instituting Proceedings).

[81] In the Tunis-Morocco Nationality Decrees case (PCIJ, *Publications,* Series B, No. 4) in which the Court held in an advisory opinion that the

Nevertheless, a determination of such rights and duties by an authoritative judicial tribunal may be of considerable value in clarifying the issues and indicating the legal nature of the concessions that may have to be made for the sake of reaching agreement. An advisory opinion may help by eliminating further controversy over the legal aspects of a dispute, or by having a calming effect on the parties. It may also define the power of another international organ to prescribe the terms of the settlement.[82] Such, in fact, appear to

---

dispute was not, by international law, solely a matter of domestic jurisdiction under Article 15 (8) of the Covenant, France and Great Britain had agreed, in the event of this answer being given by the Court, to refer the merits of the dispute to arbitration or judicial settlement, but in fact the dispute was subsequently settled by direct negotiations between the parties. Manley O. Hudson, *The Permanent Court of International Justice, 1920-1942,* p. 514. Cf. also the statement of Secretary of State Acheson on 21 September 1949 that the United States, in the dispute over the observance of human rights in Bulgaria, Hungary and Rumania, "favored submission to the International Court of Justice of the question whether they [Bulgaria, Hungary and Rumania] were under an obligation to carry out the treaty procedures." Secretary Acheson also said "the United States as an interested party would accept as binding the view of the International Court of Justice." Official Records of the Fourth Session of the General Assembly, Plenary Meetings, Summary Records of Meeting, 20 September-10 December 1949, p. 7.

Turkey refused to accept as binding a decision of the Council of the League of Nations fixing the boundary between Turkey and Iraq which the Court (PCIJ, *Publications,* Series B, No. 12) had held would be binding under the Treaty of Lausanne; later the boundary line was drawn in accordance with a treaty which did not mention the Council's decision but in fact adopted the line laid down by the Council with a slight modification. Leland M. Goodrich, "The Nature of the Advisory Opinions of the Permanent Court of International Justice," *American Journal of International Law,* Vol. 32 (1938), pp. 750-51; League of Nations Secretariat, Information Section, *Political Activities,* Vol. II, pp. 7-51.

Rumania declared in advance that the Court's advisory opinion on the Jurisdiction of the European Commission of the Danube (PCIJ, *Publications,* Series B, No. 14) would not be binding (although she agreed that the question should be referred to the Court), and subsequently refused to give full effect to it. Leland M. Goodrich, *op. cit.,* p. 752 and documents there cited; Manley O. Hudson, *op. cit.,* p. 518.

82 Two opinions dealt with the question of the finality of the decisions of the Conference of Ambassadors: one, with the question of the binding effect of the League Council's decision under the Treaty of Lausanne, and with the procedure by which it was to be reached; one, with the question whether a dispute was by international law solely a matter of domestic jurisdiction; two, with the question whether the League had competence under the minority treaties to deal with certain matters; and one with the functions of the Mixed Commission for the Exchange of Greek and Turkish Populations. PCIJ, *Publications,* Series B, Nos. 8, 9, 12, 4, 6, 7, 16. Cf. ICJ Reports 1950, p. 221.

have been the principal functions of the advisory opinions in the settlement of disputes. In most of the cases, the opinions were accepted by the interested states as elements in the settlements, but the legal relations defined by the opinions were supplemented or modified by agreement. In some cases, where the powers and procedures of international organs were involved, action was taken by the organs concerned on the basis of the opinions, but in other cases the opinions had little practical effect, since the controversies were ended by direct negotiations between the interested states.[83]

The fact that the final settlement of a dispute is not identical with the result which would follow from merely giving effect to an advisory opinion does not necessarily mean that the states or international organs concerned deny that the Court has correctly interpreted the law. "As the Court itself has recognized, even states bound by a judgment are 'always free to dispose of their rights.' "[84] States, like individuals, sometimes find it desirable to enter into agreements whereby they renounce in whole or in part their legal rights, privileges or powers. A state may "dispose of its rights" either by specifically consenting to a settlement in which it gives up something to which it is legally entitled or by empowering another state or an international organ to prescribe with binding effect the terms of a settlement which need not be in accordance with the legal relations of the parties. In either case, the state concerned adopts the policy of not insisting

---

[83] Two opinions on questions which arose in the work of the Mixed Commission for the Exchange of Greek and Turkish Populations appear to have had practically no effect on the settlements arrived at by negotiations between the parties. See Leland M. Goodrich, *op. cit.*, p. 749. In the Mosul boundary case, the action of the Council of the League, despite the supporting opinion of the Court, was not recognized as legally binding by Turkey, but undoubtedly exerted influence on the terms of the final settlement. See fn. 00 above. For reviews and discussions of the effects of the advisory opinions of PCIJ, see Manley O. Hudson, *The Permanent Court of International Justice, 1920-1942,* pp. 513-24, and Leland M. Goodrich, *op. cit., passim.*

[84] Manley O. Hudson, "The Effect of Advisory Opinions of the World Court," *American Journal of International Law,* Vol. 42 (1948), p. 631, citing PCIJ, *Publications,* Series A, No. 24, p. 11; Series A/B, No. 46, p. 153.

on its full legal rights and recognizes that other factors may be properly taken into account in reaching an adjustment most likely to put an end to the difficulties between the parties. Such an adjustment may be more conducive to the maintenance of international peace and security than insistence on legal rights.[85]

It may be noted that in a great majority of cases advisory opinions relating to existing disputes were requested by international organs with the consent of the interested states and sometimes at their behest.[86] There were only three cases before the old Court in which requests were made without such consent. In one, that of Eastern Carelia, the Court refused to give an opinion, and in another, that of the Mosul boundary, Turkey refused to give formal effect to the opinion. Only one of the requests for advisory opinions addressed to the new Court was in terms related to a concrete controversy between states, namely, the request for the interpretation of the peace treaties with Bulgaria, Hungary and Rumania.[87] In this case, Bulgaria, Hungary and Rumania had not given their consent to the request and subsequently failed to comply with the opinion. The controversy remained unsettled.[88] It may be concluded that advisory opinions are likely to be somewhat more effective as aids in the settlement of disputes when they are requested with the consent of all the interested states.

Although advisory opinions, as has been indicated, do not generally have a formal binding effect, it is possible for states and international organs to agree in advance to give them such effect. A number of international instruments provide that advisory opinions will be requested by the international

---

85 Unless it amounts to a ratification of results achieved by violence or threat of violence, in which case, even though the immediate consequence may be the preservation of peace, international security is likely to be impaired, since resort to violence is rewarded.

86 For the PCIJ cases, see Leland M. Goodrich, *op. cit.*, pp. 750 and 751.

87 ICJ Reports 1950, p. 65.

88 See p. 93.

organs concerned in disputes to which they are parties and that such opinions will be binding.[89]

Since only states may appear as parties in contentious cases before the Court, the acceptance of advisory opinions as binding provides a convenient means for the settlement of disputes between an international organ and a state, or between two international organs. It may be noted, however, that the Court has not generally been called upon to deal with questions of fact in its advisory opinions, even under the old Statute, which provided for advisory opinions on "disputes and questions." Although it has been suggested that the expression "legal question" used in the new Statute may possibly include a question as to "the existence of any fact which, if established, would constitute a breach of an international obligation" (the language used in Article 36 of the Statute with reference to the acceptance by states of the compulsory jurisdiction of the Court), the point is not settled.[90]

Although the Court has the power to refuse to give an

---

89 Thus, Section 30 of the Convention on the Privileges and Immunities of the United Nations provides that if a difference arises out of the interpretation or application of the Convention between the United Nations on the one hand and a Member on the other hand, "a request shall be made for an advisory opinion on any legal question involved in accordance with Article 96 of the Charter and Article 65 of the Statute of the Court. The opinion given by the Court shall be accepted as decisive by the parties." A similar provision is found in Section 32 of the Convention on the Privileges and Immunities of the Specialized Agencies. See also Article 96 of the Havana Charter for an International Trade Organization, and Section 21 of the Headquarters Agreement between the United Nations and the United States. Cf. Article 37 (2) of the Constitution of the International Labour Organisation. See, in this connection, Seymour J. Rubin, "The Judicial Review Problem in the International Trade Organization," *Harvard Law Review,* Vol. 63 (1949), p. 78.

90 See Manley O. Hudson, "The Twenty-Fourth Year of the World Court," *op. cit.,* p. 13; but cf. F. Blaine Sloan, "Advisory Jurisdiction of the International Court of Justice," *California Law Review,* Vol. 27 (1950), p. 841. On the problem of the extent to which advisory opinions might have dealt with questions of fact under the old Statute, see Manley O. Hudson, *The Permanent Court of International Justice, 1920-1942,* p. 498; Hans Kaufmann, *Die Gutachten des Ständigen Internationalen Gerichtshofes als Mittel zwischenstaatlicher Streitschlichtung* (Basel, Helbing und Lichtenhahn, 1939), p. 150. It is hardly possible to maintain that the Court may give an advisory opinion *ex aequo et bono.* The scope of the Court's advisory function is thus more restricted than that of its function in contentious cases.

advisory opinion, it is not likely to exercise this power lightly. The primary responsibility for the choice of questions submitted to the Court remains with the political organs. A question which is legal in form may be sometimes appropriately left to political determination. In the Austro-German Customs Regime case,[91] for example, the issue whether the customs union compromised "the independence" of Austria in contravention of international obligations was legal in form, but it is doubtful whether its submission to the Court was wise. It may be noted that the Supreme Court of the United States has held that the question which of the two opposing governments of a state of the Union was the legitimate one was to be answered by the political, rather than the judicial, branch of the federal government, and that the constitutional guarantee to every state of a republican form of government raised a political question which the Supreme Court could not decide.[92] Only a political decision is likely to be fruitful in such cases. Realistic recognition of the burden imposed upon the Court by the question whether a state's "independence" is impaired by an international arrangement such as a customs union, should have led to a similar result.[93]

The disputes in the settlement or attempted settlement of which the advisory opinions of the Court have played a role have on the whole been more "political" in nature than the disputes submitted to the Court as contentious cases; some of them were symptomatic of generally unfriendly relations between the states concerned, as for instance the dispute over railway traffic between Lithuania and Poland;[94] and in some, passions were aroused which might have led to serious de-

---

91 PCIJ, *Publications,* Series A/B, No. 41. See also p. 53 above.

92 *Luther v. Borden,* 7 How. 1 (1849); see also *Taylor v. Beckham,* 178 U.S. 548, 578 (1900) and *Pacific States Telephone & Telegraph Co. v. Oregon,* 223 U.S. 118 (1912).

93 See Grant Gilmore, *op. cit.,* p. 1056.

94 PCIJ, *Publications,* Series A/B, No. 42. For a brief account of the unsuccessful efforts of the League Council to improve relations between Lithuania and Poland, see James T. Shotwell and Marina Salvin, *Lessons on Security and Disarmament from the History of the League of Nations* (New York, Carnegie Endowment for International Peace, 1949), pp. 62-63.

terioration in the relations between the states concerned in the absence of a satisfactory settlement.[95]

The efforts of the League of Nations to maintain peace were undoubtedly aided to some extent by the opportunity to refer legal questions to the Court, although not all the disputes were ended by lasting settlements on the basis of the Court's opinions.[96] However, no advisory opinions were asked of the Court by the organs of the League after 23 September 1935.[97] From the summer of 1935 on, the international security situation deteriorated rapidly, and the world was faced with a series of major crises. When the half-hearted attempt to stop the Italo-Ethiopian War by economic sanctions failed, the prestige and authority of the League declined, and appeasement was tried as a means of preventing a general war. In these circumstances, purely political settlements were sought with which the Court had nothing to do.

Use of the Court By the United Nations

Have the organs of the United Nations made effective use of the advisory function of the Court?

---

95 An early instance in which the use of the Court apparently contributed to the calming of passions was the Jaworzina boundary dispute between Poland and Czechoslovakia in 1923, in which the Council of the League, at the behest of the two governments concerned, requested an advisory opinion on a legal question and subsequently provided for final settlement in accordance with the opinion. PCIJ, *Publications,* Series B, No. 8; League of Nations Secretariat, Information Section, *Political Activities,* Vol. I, pp. 88-92; Manley O. Hudson, *The Permanent Court of International Justice, 1920-1942,* p. 524; A. Hammarskjöld, *op. cit.,* pp. 457 and 469.

96 In this connection, reference may also be made to the Aaland Islands dispute between Finland and Sweden which stirred up strong feelings and fears of hostilities between the two countries but was successfully settled by the Council of the League in 1921 after what amounted to an advisory opinion had been given by a Commission of Jurists to the effect that the dispute was not a matter solely within the domestic jurisdiction of Finland, and that treaty provisions on the demilitarization of the islands were still in force. At that time the Court was not yet in existence and the function performed by the Commission was very similar to the advisory function of the Court. See League of Nations Secretariat, Information Section, *Political Activities,* Vol. I, pp. 7-23.

97 On that date an opinion on the consistency of certain Danzig legislative decrees with the constitution of the Free City was requested by the Council. See PCIJ, *Publications,* Series A/B, No. 65.

Although the Council of the League had never asked the Court for an interpretation of the League Covenant in abstract terms, and doubt had been expressed of the propriety of such action,[98] the General Assembly of the United Nations has addressed several requests to the Court for an interpretation of the Charter.[99] Some of these requests were couched in abstract terms, but were actually made as a result of concrete differences between the Members of the United Nations as to the application of the Charter, of which the Court was well aware. The first request raised the question whether a Member of the United Nations, in voting on the admission of a state to membership in the United Nations, is juridically entitled to make its consent to the admission dependent on conditions not expressly provided by Article 4 (1) of the Charter, and in particular on the condition that other states be admitted to membership. The decision to submit this question to the Court grew out of the debates in the General Assembly concerning the refusal of the Soviet Union to support in the Security Council the admission of certain states. The answer of the Court, given by a majority of nine to six, was in the negative, but had no visible effect on the Soviet position, and it is difficult to see what effect it could have, since a Member of the United Nations is not required to state the reasons for its votes in the political organs. Nothing was gained by the submission of this question to the Court.[100] Motives cannot be judicially controlled.

The request for an opinion on the competence of the General Assembly in the matter of admission of new Members likewise grew out of the deadlock produced by Soviet

---

98 See Manley O. Hudson, *The Permanent Court of International Justice, 1920-1942,* p. 498.

99 Admission of a State to the United Nations, ICJ Reports 1948, p. 57; Competence of Assembly Regarding Admission to the United Nations, ICJ Reports 1950, p. 4. Interpretation of the Charter was also involved in the advisory opinions on Reparation for Injuries Suffered in the Service of the United Nations, ICJ Reports 1949, p. 174, and International Status of South West Africa, ICJ Reports 1950, p. 128.

100 There is no indication that the opinion gave any substantial political or moral advantage to the Western nations over the Soviet bloc. The answer of the Court was supported by rather involved reasoning shared by seven of

vetoes in the Security Council. Some of the smaller nations, led by Argentina, asserted that the General Assembly could admit new members even when the Security Council had made no recommendation for admission. The question whether the Assembly had such power was submitted to the Court. On this question the United States and the Soviet Union found themselves on the same side. The negative answer of the Court, supported by twelve of the judges, confirmed the practice which had actually prevailed and may have been useful in eliminating further futile debate on the matter.

The Soviet Union has generally opposed the reference to the Court of questions by the political organs of the United Nations, and has challenged the competence of the Court to interpret the Charter, but its spokesmen have on occasion cited with approval the advisory opinions favorable to the Soviet position.[101] Although the Soviet member of the Court has not given explicit support to the Soviet contention that the Court is incompetent to interpret the Charter, he has pointed out that the Permanent Court of International Justice was never asked to give an abstract interpretation of the Covenant, and has taken the view that the Court should refuse to give such an interpretation of the Charter.[102]

It is too early to appraise the consequences of the practice of asking the Court to interpret the Charter in abstract terms. In general, it is worthy of note that in the League system it was the Council, the organ which most frequently handled international disputes, that made all the requests for advisory opinions, while in the United Nations system,

---

the judges and the even more involved reasoning of two concurring judges which was interpreted by Soviet spokesmen as virtually depriving the answer of its apparent meaning. See the speech of A. Vyshinsky on 8 December 1948, Official Records of the Third Session of the General Assembly, Part I, pp. 795-96, and S. Borisov, "Priem Novykh Chlenov v Organizatsiiu Ob'edinennykh Natsii," *Sovetskoe Gosudarstvo i Pravo,* 1948, No. 9, p. 6. Cf. Manley O. Hudson, "The Twenty-Seventh Year of the World Court," *American Journal of International Law,* Vol. 43 (1949), pp. 10-11.

101 See, *e.g.,* General Assembly, Official Records: Fifth Session, *Ad Hoc* Political Committee, 5th Meeting, 5 October 1950, pp. 26-27.

102 ICJ Reports 1948, pp. 107-09.

on the contrary, all such requests have so far come from the General Assembly.

As previously indicated, the attitude of the parties is a limiting factor on the usefulness of advisory opinions in the settlement of disputes. Thus, despite the advisory opinion, to which reference has already been made, given by the Court at the request of the General Assembly to the effect that disputes existed under the peace treaties with Bulgaria, Hungary and Rumania, and that the latter states were obligated to carry out the provisions of the peace treaties relating to the settlement of disputes, including the provisions for the appointment of their representatives to the treaty commissions, the three ex-enemy states concerned have continued to refuse to take the necessary steps.[103] Under the circumstances, little was gained by making the request for an advisory opinion, and it might have been better for the Court in order to safeguard its prestige to follow the precedent of the Eastern Carelia case and refuse to give an opinion on the ground that Bulgaria, Hungary and Rumania were not members of the United Nations and had objected to the proceedings.[104]

It is not yet clear whether the advisory opinion on the international status of South West Africa, in which the Court held that the Union of South Africa continues to have international obligations under the mandate, that the United Nations is entitled to exercise supervisory functions over the administration of the mandate, and that the Union acting alone is not competent to modify the international status of

---

[103] ICJ Reports 1950, pp. 65 and 221; Resolution of the General Assembly, 3 November 1950, General Assembly, Official Records: Fifth Session, Supplement No. 20 (A/1775), Resolutions Adopted by the General Assembly, during the Period 19 September to 15 December 1950, p. 16. Subsequently, the Court held by eleven votes to two that the Secretary-General of the United Nations was not authorized to appoint the third member of a treaty commission if one party failed to appoint its representative to the Commission. ICJ Reports 1950, p. 221.

[104] See p. 19 above. It is possible that the opinion had some "value" for the purpose of creating the impression that something was being done about the alleged violations of the human rights provisions of the peace treaties, since in some quarters there were demands for action by the United Nations, although it was fairly evident that no effective action was feasible.

the territory, will have any effect on the conduct of the government of the Union.[105]

The new Court has not yet been called upon to interpret any of the multilateral conventions in the economic, social and technical fields. In the old Court, by contrast, the first three advisory opinions dealt with questions which had arisen under the constitution of the International Labour Organisation, and several other opinions also concerned the powers and activities of non-political international organs. Yet in the League system only the Council and the Assembly had the power to ask for advisory opinions, while under the Charter such power may also be given by the General Assembly to the non-political organs of the United Nations and specialized agencies. It has in fact been conferred upon, with some limitations, the Economic and Social Council, the Trusteeship Council, and nine specialized agencies, as well as upon the Interim Committee of the General Assembly.

Suggestions for the submission of certain questions to the Court are frequently made, with varying degrees of earnestness, in the course of debates in the various United Nations bodies. The Security Council rejected a proposal that its competence to act in the Indonesian situation be tested by referring to the Court the question whether the situation was a matter "essentially within the domestic jurisdiction of a state," and proposals of a similar nature were rejected by the General Assembly in connection with the question of the treatment of Indians in South Africa and the problem of Palestine.[106] In view of the emotions aroused by the problems involved, these decisions may have been wise, par-

---

105 ICJ Reports 1950, p. 128; Resolution of the General Assembly, 13 December 1950, General Assembly, Official Records: Fifth Session, Supplement No. 20, p. 55.

106 See Leland M. Goodrich, "The United Nations and Domestic Jurisdiction," *International Organization,* Vol. III (1949), p. 14, Report of the Sub-Committee on International Cooperation in the Political Field to the Interim Committee, United Nations Doc. A/AC.18/114, 5 July 1950, pp. 58-61; L. Larry Leonard, "The United Nations and Palestine," *International Conciliation,* No. 454 (October, 1949), pp. 642-43, 658 and 690-91; J. Foster Collins, "The United Nations and Indonesia," *ibid.,* No. 459 (March, 1950), p. 128n.

ticularly if the political organs concerned were determined to act regardless of the opinion of the Court. Yet it may be remembered that the Council of the League of Nations on two occasions asked for advisory opinions on the question of domestic jurisdiction — in the Aaland Islands case (where the request for the opinion was addressed to a Commission of Jurists), and in the Tunis-Morocco Nationality Decrees case — without any detrimental effect on its authority or on the position of the Court. It has been well said that "where opinions among Members differ upon the interpretation of the Charter and legal doubts as to the Assembly's competence are strongly and sincerely held, the force of a recommendation by the Assembly will be weakened if it is made without an affirmative decision upon the question of competence preferably with the assistance of the International Court of Justice in cases where it is practicable."[107] This applies to the Security Council no less than to the General Assembly. Lack of certainty as to the competence of the political organs concerned hampered United Nations action in both the Palestinian[108] and the Indonesian situations.[109]

Should States Be Empowered to Ask for Advisory Opinions?

Proposals have been made from time to time that the power to request advisory opinions be conferred on states.[110] The consequences of the adoption of such a proposal are difficult to estimate. It might make states less willing to accept the jurisdiction of the Court with binding effect.

---

107 Report of the Sub-Committee on International Co-operation in the Political Field to the Interim Committee, United Nations Doc. A/AC.18/114, 5 July 1950, p. 61.

108 See L. Larry Leonard, *op. cit.*

109 "The problem of jurisdiction haunted the Council for the next two years and considerably hampered its freedom of action." J. Foster Collins, *op. cit.*, p. 127. For a criticism of the Security Council's failure to obtain an advisory opinion, see Louis B. Wehle, "The United Nations By-Passes the International Court as the Council's Adviser, A Study in Contrived Frustration," *University of Pennsylvania Law Review*, Vol. 98 (1950), p. 285.

110 In 1920 such a proposal was made by Argentina. See Manley O. Hudson, *The Permanent Court of International Justice, 1920-1942*, p. 486.

Should advisory opinions be given at the request of states and disregarded by them, the Court's authority would be impaired. Should the states agree in advance or develop a uniform policy to give effect to the opinions, they would amount to judgments in a different form. The advisory opinions of the Court are often useful in the work of international organs, but there is danger of diluting the tribunal's authority by an undue extension of its advisory functions.

A Power of Judicial Review?

At the San Francisco Conference, Belgium proposed that a state be given the power to request an advisory opinion on the question whether its "essential rights" were infringed by a recommendation or decision of the Security Council. In case of an affirmative answer, the Security Council would be obliged to reconsider its action or refer the matter to the General Assembly for decision. This proposal was supported by Colombia but opposed by the great powers and failed of adoption.[111]

It is to be doubted whether much would be gained in the formative stage of world organization by placing the action of an already weak Security Council under the control of an even weaker Court. A clash between the Council and the Court might be fatal to both. Yet an organization whose various organs and members all have the power to interpret the basic constitutional instrument without definite legal effect on the other organs and members can hardly be viable. At present, the weakness of the organization largely protects its members from abuse of power. If the organization is to gain strength, the authority to give binding interpretations of the Charter, at least in matters directly affecting the rights

---

In 1944 the Informal Inter-Allied Committee on the Future of the Permanent Court of International Justice recommended that such power be conferred on two or more states acting in concert, and in 1945 Venezuela made a similar proposal which was rejected at the San Francisco Conference. See U. S. Department of State, *The International Court of Justice: Selected Documents Relating to the Drafting of the Statute,* Publication 2491 (1946), pp. 51 and 86; UNCIO *Documents,* Vol. XIII, pp. 235 and 496.

[111] See Hans Kelsen, *op. cit.,* p. 446n., and documents there cited.

and duties of states, must be lodged somewhere, preferably in a judicial organ. The long-range purposes and policies laid down in the Charter must be given some protection against the possible short-range aberrations of the political organs. Power without law is despotism.[112] But the efficacy of the protection exercised by a judicial organ is, of course, in the last analysis always dependent on the support of the dominant part of the community.

Extrajudicial Activity of the Court

The existence of the Court has contributed to the settlement of some disputes, both legal and non-legal in character, in a way not envisaged in the Statute. Numerous international treaties and agreements have contained provisions calling for the appointment of arbitrators or other persons with international functions by the Court or one of its members (usually the President). The Court or its members have on many occasions complied with the requests to make such appointments. For example, in 1931 the Court appointed members of the Czechoslovak-Hungarian, Hungarian-Rumanian and Hungarian-Yugoslav Mixed Arbitral Tribunals; in 1949 the President of the Court appointed three members of a Rumanian-Swiss permanent conciliation commission and the president of an arbitral tribunal of Unesco, while the Vice President, at the request of the French government, appointed observers to ensure the impartiality of a referendum in the French Settlements in India on the question of the future status of the Settlements.[113]

The readiness of the Court to assume this function, which must be regarded as extrajudicial, has been criticized, but

112 See John Foster Dulles, *War or Peace* (New York, Macmillan Co., 1950), p. 198.

113 For these and many other instances, see the Annual Reports (*Publications,* Series E) of PCIJ and the Yearbooks of ICJ; see also Manley O. Hudson, *The Permanent Court of International Justice, 1920-1942,* pp. 433-34.

does not seem to have had any untoward consequences. It must, of course, be exercised with caution and in the same spirit of impartiality as the judicial functions of the Court.

An Appraisal

In the total picture of the international relations of the last thirty years the contribution of the Court to peace through the settlement of disputes does not loom large. The disputes which in fact were most dangerous to the peace of the world never reached the Court. No attempt was made to use the Court to resolve the clashes of interest which led to the great armed conflicts during the period of the Court's existence — the Sino-Soviet hostilities in 1929, the Chaco War between Bolivia and Paraguay, the Japanese military action in Manchuria and China, the war between Italy and Ethiopia, the civil war in Spain and the foreign intervention which accompanied it, the second World War, the war between Finland and the Soviet Union in 1939-1940, the fighting in Indonesia, Palestine, Hyderabad and Kashmir since 1945, or the armed conflict which began in 1950 in Korea.

Furthermore, many of the less serious conflicts in which armed force was used or threatened to be used were settled in whole or in part by or with the aid of international organs through political procedures without reference to the Court. This was true of the dispute between Poland and Lithuania over Vilna in 1922, the bombardment of Corfu by Italy in 1923, the seizure of Memel by the Lithuanians in 1923, the armed clash between Greece and Bulgaria in 1925, the Leticia dispute between Colombia and Peru in 1932-1934, incidents between Hungary and Yugoslavia in 1934, the dispute over Alexandretta between France and Turkey in 1936-1939, the situations in Indonesia and Palestine, the "Berlin blockade" in 1948-1949, and incidents in Central America and the Caribbean in 1948-1950. Some of these "settlements" (for example Vilna and Corfu) amounted to little more than ratifications of results obtained by the use of force and were hardly conducive to the development of a sense of general security; others (for instance Leticia) were more substantial contributions to the cause of peace with justice.[114]

During the interwar period, at least thirty of the judgments and advisory opinions given by the Court were directly related to some phase of the peace settlement after the first World War, not counting the six advisory opinions which concerned the powers and activities of the International Labour Organisation.[115] Although the Court, in a larger sense, was itself a product of that settlement, and had to function within the framework of the *status quo* established at Versailles, the interests of the states defeated in the war (including Danzig) and their nationals or former nationals were given protection in many of these cases. In particular, the interests of the German minority in Poland were given protection against Polish pretensions in a majority of the cases in which they were involved. The Court not only thus demonstrated its judicial independence and impartiality, but was also instrumental in alleviating the lot of the defeated and presumably in reducing the tensions growing out of the first World War. But the Court's opinion adverse to the proposed customs union between Austria and Germany, although given two days after the states concerned an-

---

114 During the same period, a number of disputes connected with the use or possible use of force were referred to tribunals other than the Court. Several boundary disputes in Latin America were submitted to arbitration, but not all the awards were carried out. The Chaco War was concluded by a peace treaty which left the territorial dispute between Bolivia and Paraguay to be settled *ex aequo et bono* by the heads of six American republics. The award was not based on standards of international law and was undoubtedly influenced by the power relation which prevailed between the parties at the close of the hostilities. The dispute which arose out of the sinking of the Canadian vessel *I'm Alone* by the United States Coast Guard was settled by Commissioners appointed by the two governments in a proceeding akin to arbitration. The arbitration of the Wal Wal incident between Italy and Ethiopia was a minor incident in the developments which culminated in the Italo-Ethiopian war. See, for these and other cases, United Nations, *Reports of International Arbitral Awards,* pp. 223, 921, 1011, 1307, 1609, 1657 and 1817.

115 Thirteen of the cases involved questions of the treatment of minorities and exchanges of population, eight related to boundary questions and the use of international waterways, six dealt with Danzig and its relations with Poland, and three were of miscellaneous character.

nounced the abandonment of the plan, did not contribute to better feelings between Germany and the French bloc and overshadowed the decisions favorable to German interests in less spectacular cases. It is, of course, a matter of history that the discontent of the defeated nations, and particularly of Germany, became a powerful factor in the outbreak of the second World War.

The immediate effect of the Court's activity as an organ for the settlement of disputes has not been spectacular. It would be difficult to maintain that any judgment or advisory opinion of the Court had the specific effect of preventing recourse to violence in an international dispute. Even in the Corfu Channel case the settlement of the dispute by the Court was probably not the decisive factor in averting further violence.

It would be difficult to deny, on the other hand, that the use of the Court has in some instances contributed to the relaxation of tension between the contestants and may have prevented further deterioration in relations between them. The Corfu Channel dispute, for example, was effectively taken out of the arena of world politics by its submission to the Court; it ceased to be a subject of mutual recrimination in public statements and in the press; in particular, it disappeared as another symbol of the widening gulf between the Soviet bloc and the West. No veto interfered with its adjudication by the Court. The difficulties encountered by the United Kingdom in the collection of the damages awarded by the Court have virtually escaped public notice. Nor did the judgment of the Court, on the whole unfavorable to Albania, become a butt for Communist propaganda and for accusations of imperialist bullying. The prestige of a decision by the Court may in part account for this result. In many other cases the calm atmosphere and the moral prestige of a judicial settlement may be reasonably assumed to have had a pacifying effect.

Through its judgments and advisory opinions the tribunal has contributed to the elimination or reduction of some tensions which might not have led to war, but which might have poisoned the atmosphere of relations between otherwise friendly nations. In this fashion, it has facilitated cooperation between states. It has made easier, by resolving some troublesome problems, the formation of groups of states determined to strengthen general security by resisting aggression and threats of aggression.[116]

The real significance of the Court's work lies in its long-range effect. A start has been made in the right direction. For the first time in history, adjudication of disputes between states by a standing international tribunal with world-wide functions has become a reality. Further progress must of necessity be slow. Those who expect miracles or believe in panaceas are usually disappointed. It has been pointed out that it took over fifty years to get the states of the Union to accept the decisions of the Supreme Court of the United States on boundary questions; "it was over eighty years before any other question of importance [between states] was submitted for its decision."[117] The growth of international jurisdiction cannot be much faster.

Effective adjudication of international disputes on an obligatory basis cannot be expected to become a significant reality in the immediate future. It must be supported by the development of a sentiment of world community and a determination to uphold the rule of law in relations between states which are today largely lacking. It is indeed doubtful whether judicial settlement of disputes between states will ever be a factor of prime importance in the maintenance of world peace. It is much more likely to be a by-product of

116 In this connection it may be noted that the submission to the Court in 1950 of the question whether United States nationals are entitled to certain preferential treatment in French Morocco under treaties in force followed upon the adoption by Congress of an amendment to the ERP appropriation act for 1950 directing the withholding of funds "to any nation of which a dependent area fails, in the opinion of the President, to comply with any treaty to which the United States and such dependent area are parties." This amendment was adopted as a result of the complaints of certain United States businessmen that their opportunities in French Morocco were being limited by trade restrictions imposed in violation of United States treaty rights. See Department of State *Bulletin*, Vol. 23 (1950), p. 950.

117 Charles Warren, *op. cit.*, p. 40.

the gradual transference of effective power and authority over individuals from the governments of the particular states to a supra-national agency. But the extension of the practice of referring disputes to the Court may help to shape the attitudes and habits necessary for such a transference. Frequent resort to the Court for the settlement of even seemingly unimportant controversies is likely to contribute to the development of patterns of thought and action essential for the peaceful coexistence of states and to strengthen the feeling that international law should be obeyed.

Until the United Nations develops the power and the determination to enforce the judgments of the Court and to give effect to advisory opinions, the usefulness of the Court remains dependent on the willingness of states to comply with such judgments and opinions. The very good record of compliance with the Court's decisions must be attributed in large part to the voluntary acceptance of the Court's jurisdiction. Efforts to impose the authority of the Court upon states not willing to submit to it, either in contentious cases or in advisory proceedings, run the risk of seriously harming the prestige and usefulness of the Court by increasing the frequency with which its decisions are disregarded. Wider acceptance of the jurisdiction of the Court is highly desirable, but, in the present stage of world organization, it must be voluntary.[118]

The effective utilization of the Court thus depends primarily on the policies of the governments concerned. The Court must not be misused for propaganda purposes. The scope of its activities can be gradually extended without impairment of its authority by cautious but consistent policies of submitting to it as many appropriate cases as possible and by keeping it free of the burden of dealing with matters primarily political in character. The leading states of the world whose announced goal is a world rule of law have the primary responsibility for the development of such policies.

---

118 See, in this connection, Grant Gilmore, *op. cit.*

IV. THE COURT AND THE ENFORCEMENT OF PEACE

International law can help reduce tensions and contribute to the preservation of peace only when the states concerned want to use it for this purpose. When a state is prepared to resort to armed force to get what it wants, it can be restrained, if at all, only by superior power. The enforcement of peace is, under Chapter VII of the Charter of the United Nations, a responsibility of the Security Council. As already pointed out, the Council has the power, though not the duty, to take measures to give effect to the judgments of the Court; it also has the power, without prior or subsequent recourse to the Court, to determine that a threat to the peace, a breach of the peace or an act of aggression exists, and to decide upon the measures necessary to maintain or restore international peace and security. The Security Council may, in its discretion, request an advisory opinion of the Court on any legal question that may arise in the performance of its functions, but the Council's decisions are not judicially reviewable as of right. The seemingly vast and ill-defined powers of the Security Council are in reality very much limited by the requirement of the unanimity of its permanent members for action on other than procedural matters and by the lack of obligation on the part of the Members of the United Nations to supply military forces to carry out the Council's decisions in the absence of a special agreement.

At present the Court has very little to do with the enforcement of peace. Can it play a greater role in the future? Suggestions for expanding the functions of the Court in this connection may be divided into those which favor judicial review of the actions of the political organs of the United Nations, and those which envisage a system of world security based on judicial determinations of the breaches of the law.

Reference has already been made to the Belgian proposal to give the Court a measure of control over the actions of the Security Council, and considerations for and against such control have been pointed out.[1] These considerations apply with particular force to the coercive functions of the United Nations. At the present stage it is hardly desirable to inhibit the Security Council still further by provisions for judicial review of its actions. A strong Security Council, however, might be tempted to take arbitrary action against certain states without regard for their legal rights unless restrained by another organ.[2] It may be pointed out, in this connection, that while judicial review of *legislative* action is by no means universally adopted in modern states,[3] there is some measure of judicial protection for the individual against abuses of power by the police and other administrative agencies in all civilized communities. The Security Council as a peace-enforcement organ is comparable to such administrative agencies rather than to legislative organs. Serious attention should, therefore, be given to the problem of judicial review of the actions of the Security Council when the latter attains greater strength.

Of the proposals to make judicial decisions the basis for the enforcement of peace perhaps the most notable is that of Kelsen.[4] Under this proposal, it would be the duty of the Council of the world organization to enforce the orders of an international court and to apply the necessary sanctions against a state which has been held by the court to have violated the covenant.

---

1 See above pp. 96-97.

2 The effectiveness of the restraint would, of course, depend on the relative prestige of such organ and the Security Council.

3 It is significant, however, that in many *federal* states (*i.e.*, in states where the long-range policy is to divide legislative and executive authority between the central government and the governments of subordinate entities) some measure of judicial control over legislation is entrusted to the courts. There is an obvious analogy between a federal state and a world community with a strong international security organization.

4 Hans Kelsen, *Peace Through Law* (Chapel Hill, University of North Carolina Press, 1944).

There is no doubt that such proposals have much apparent merit. Historical experience indicates that order and law are inseparable. They are two sides of the same coin. The orderliness of behavior depends on the existence of known standards of behavior, but the latter do not really exist unless they are reasonably well-observed in practice.[5] One of the functions of law is to channel individual conduct into socially desirable directions by making fairly certain that unpleasant consequences will follow deviations from the prescribed standards. The sense of security that prevails in a well-organized community is indissolubly linked with the predictability of such consequences and with the definiteness of the standards sought to be enforced. The interpretation and application of such standards by a relatively independent and impartial judicial tribunal, rather than by political organs swayed by considerations which may be irrelevant to the long-range policy of the community, enhances their definiteness and the certainty of their enforcement. A system of enforcement of law based on judicial decisions may, therefore, be considered as normally superior to a system of peace enforcement based on political decisions alone. Security against aggression cannot be assured if the meaning of aggression is indefinite and sanctions uncertain.

The primary purpose of the United Nations must be to *prevent* violence rather than to stop violence after it has begun. This purpose may often be best accomplished by putting the potential troublemaker on notice that punishment will surely follow the transgression. But this requires a common understanding of what is forbidden.

In modern criminal codes, various crimes are defined with different degrees of specificity, and the statutory definitions are supplemented by judicial interpretations. It may be

---

[5] Professor Brierly's view that order must precede law appears to be based on a narrow definition of "law" as a system of standards enforced by independent courts on the English model. J. L. Brierly, *The Outlook for International Law* (Oxford, The Clarendon Press, 1944), pp. 73ff. In a broader sense any authoritative regulation of behavior is law, whether it is enforced by independent tribunals or otherwise. If law in this sense is completely lacking, there is no order.

logically argued that it is no more difficult to define "aggression" than to define murder, robbery, or "disorderly conduct."[6] The concept of aggression has already been judicially applied in the trials of the major Axis war criminals by the International Military Tribunals of Nuremberg and Tokyo. Furthermore, the experience of the administration of justice in modern states indicates that there is nothing inherently slow or cumbersome about the judicial process when speed of action is required. In the International Court the hearing and decision of a contentious case usually takes many months, often well over a year, but devices similar to restraining orders or preliminary injunctions may enable an international tribunal to prevent the commission of irreparable injury before the dispute is fully adjudicated.[7]

The great weakness of the proposals to make the Court or a similar tribunal the central organ in a peace-enforcement system lies not in any technical deficiencies of judicial procedures but in the assumption that the community of states, in its present stage of development, is comparable to the communities of individuals organized into states. In the international community as we know it, effective power is held, in varying amounts, by the relatively small number of states composing it. This power rests, in the last analysis, on the loyalties of the individuals who compose the states. In such a community, states may not be expected to lend their power to the enforcement of the orders of a non-political body such

---

6 See, *e.g.*, the definition of "disorderly conduct" in New York Penal Law, § 722.

7 Article 41 of the Statute of the Court provides: "1. The Court shall have the power to indicate, if it considers that circumstances so require, any provisional measures which ought to be taken to preserve the respective rights of either party. 2. Pending the final decision, notice of the measures suggested shall forthwith be given to the parties and to the Security Council." Article 61 of the Rules of Court, which elaborates the procedure to be followed on requests for interim measures of protection, authorizes the President to take the necessary measures pending action by the Court. Interim measures of protection were taken by the PCIJ or its President on several occasions. See Manley O. Hudson, *The Permanent Court of International Justice, 1920-1942* (New York, Macmillan Co., 1943), pp. 424-30; Edward Dumbauld, "Relief *Pendente Lite* in the Permanent Court of International Justice," *American Journal of International Law,* Vol. 39 (1945), p. 391.

as a court except when their own interests demand it. For this reason the enforcement of peace must be left for the present to the political decision of the states capable of applying effective power.

It is, furthermore, doubtful whether any world organization composed of states which retain effective power and the primary loyalties of individuals can assure the maintenance of international peace and security on the basis of law by the threat or application of sanctions. The relatively small number of states composing the international community and their fixed geographical position make impersonal administration of the law much more difficult than it is in a community composed of thousands or millions of relatively similar and ambulatory individuals. States cannot escape their neighbors nor ignore their particular interests. Small nations can be coerced by stronger states into good behavior, but the application of military sanctions against a great power is itself indistinguishable from war. Even action taken against a small state may so affect the balance of power among the strong nations as to increase rather than reduce the danger of war. It is impossible to mask the true nature of the resulting conflicts by calling them "police actions."[8] A state is not a physical being; it is a system of relations among individuals. A state cannot be arrested or put in jail. Nor can a state be "punished"; sanctions against a state really strike at individuals who may or may not have anything to do with the transgression against which the sanctions are directed.[9]

The differences between a state and an individual are such that the superficially attractive analogy between a judicial proceeding against a state and a proceeding against an individual breaks down. If an individual is accused of a crime, he may be arrested and held in custody pending trial

[8] Cf. Philip C. Jessup, *A Modern Law of Nations* (New York, Macmillan Co., 1948), pp. 5 and 188-89. The events of 1950-1951 in Korea confirm this view.

[9] Cf., in this connection, F. Blaine Sloan, "Comparative International and Municipal Law Sanctions," *Nebraska Law Review*, Vol. 27 (1947), p. 1.

to ensure his presence and the execution of the sentence. His premises and belongings may be searched for incriminating evidence. No similar procedures are available against states.[10] Only an army can act as a "sheriff" against a strong state. "Interim measures of protection," no less than the final judgment, may require a virtual war for enforcement.

It does not appear that peace has ever been successfully maintained, over appreciably long periods of time, by the application of coercive sanctions to political entities alone. This fact was well known to the framers of the United States Constitution.[11] Federal force has never been used in the United States to enforce a judgment against a state of the Union, and at least one such judgment remained unexecuted.[12] Yet in most federal unions courts have compulsory jurisdiction in disputes between the states and their decisions are usually obeyed. This is attributable to the transfer of the primary allegiance of the individuals from the subordinate entities to the federal Union and to the growth of respect for law.

---

10 It may be futile, for instance, to define certain acts such as "aggression" as breaches of the law triable in a court unless the prosecuting authority is able to obtain evidence proving that certain individuals have acted as agents of the defendant state. Yet such evidence may itself be unobtainable without a major armed conflict. Much of the evidence used in the Nuremberg and Tokyo trials became available to the prosecution only after the defeat of the Axis powers.

11 Madison said: "The practicability of making laws, with coercive sanctions, for the States as political bodies, had been exploded on all hands." Max Farrand, ed., *The Records of the Federal Convention of 1787,* Vol. II, p. 9. "In an association where the general authority is confined to the collective bodies of the communities that compose it, every breach of the laws must involve a state of war; and military execution must become the only instrument of civil obedience. Such a state of things can certainly not deserve the name of Government, nor would any prudent man choose to commit his happiness to it." *The Federalist,* No. XV; see also No. XVI. See further, Harrop Freeman and Theodore Paullin, *Coercion of States: In Federal Unions* (Philadelphia, the Pacifist Research Bureau, 1943), and Edwin Borchard, "The Impracticability of 'Enforcing' Peace," *Yale Law Journal,* Vol. 55 (1946), p. 966.

12 For a thorough discussion, see James N. Rosenberg, "*Brutum Fulmen:* A Precedent for a World Court," *Columbia Law Review,* Vol. 25 (1925), p. 783. The coercion of the southern states in 1861-1865 was not undertaken to enforce a judicial decision and was successful only at the cost of a major civil war.

Peace and security can never be absolute since revolutions and civil strife occur in all communities, but international wars are likely to disappear only when effective power has been transferred from the particular states to the agencies of the world community[13] and when individuals everywhere become directly subject to world law and its organs. No "international police force" can succeed in enforcing peace until it is backed by a strong sense of the imperative character of world law.

> It is not the existence of a police force that makes a system of law strong and respected, but the strength of the law that makes it possible for a police force to be effectively organized. The imperative character of law is felt so strongly within a highly civilized state that national law has developed a machinery of enforcement which generally works smoothly, though never so smoothly as to make breaches impossible. If the imperative character of international law were equally strongly felt, the institution of definite international sanctions would easily follow.[14]

In the meantime, the International Court can play only a modest role in the maintenance of international peace and security, although through its activity it may contribute to the necessary shifts in primary allegiances and habits of thought. Yet, if the United Nations gains in strength, a corresponding growth must take place in the authority and power of the Court, if the world is to be preserved from lawless despotism and if the habit of respect for law is to prevail. All effective law must be supported by power, but the wise possessor of power knows that the latter is often best preserved by self-restraint through law.

---

13 Cf. Charles Cheney Hyde, "Bombs, Super-Bombs, and the Cost of Peace," *Texas Law Review,* Vol. 29 (1950), p. 143.

14 J. L. Brierly, *The Law of Nations* (4th ed., Oxford, The Clarendon Press, 1949), p. 73.

SELECTED BIBLIOGRAPHY

BIBLIOGRAPHIES OF THE COURT

Comprehensive annual bibliographies of publications relating to the Court and its activities have been compiled by the Registry of the Court and since 1925 printed in the Annual Reports of the Permanent Court of International Justice (Publications, Series E), and in the Yearbooks of the International Court of Justice. They have also been released as separate pamphlets.

PUBLICATIONS OF THE COURT

International Court of Justice. *Reports of Judgments, Advisory Opinions and Orders.* Short title: I.C.J. Reports (year).

———. *Pleadings, Oral Arguments, Documents.* Short title: I.C.J. Pleadings.

———. *Documents Concerning the Organization of the Court* (1946,1947).

———. *Yearbooks.*

Permanent Court of International Justice. *Publications.* Series A. Judgments and Orders. Nos. 1 to 24 (1922-1930).

———. Series B. Advisory Opinions. Nos. 1 to 18 (1922-1930).

———. Series A/B. Judgments, Orders and Advisory Opinions. Nos. 40 to 80 (1931-1940).

———. Series C. Acts and Documents Relating to Judgments and Advisory Opinions. Nos. 1-19, 52-87 (1922-1939).

———. Series D. Acts and Documents Concerning the Organization of the Court. Nos. 1 to 6 (1922-1940).

———. Series E. Annual Reports. Nos. 1 to 15 (1925-1939).

———. Series F. General Indexes. Nos. 1 to 4 (1922-1936).

OTHER DOCUMENTS

Great Britain, Parliamentary Papers, Miscellaneous No. 12 (1929), *Memorandum on the Signature by His Majesty's Government in the United Kingdom of the Optional Clause of the Statute of the Permanent Court of International Justice,* Cmd. 3452.

————. Miscellaneous No. 2 (1944), *Report of the Informal Inter-Allied Committee on the Future of the Permanent Court of International Justice, 10 February 1944,* Cmd. 6531.

HUDSON, MANLEY O., editor. *World Court Reports: A Collection of the judgments, Orders and Opinions of the Permanent Court of International Justice.* 4 vols. Washington, Carnegie Endowment for International Peace, 1934-1943.

League of Nations. Records of the First Assembly, Meetings of Committees.

————. Secretariat, Information Section. *Political Activities.* 2 vols. [1925, 1928]

United Nations. General Assembly. Official Records of the Second Session. Plenary Meetings, 16 September–29 November 1947.

————. Official Records of the Second Session. Resolutions, 16 September–29 November 1947.

————. Official Records of the Third Session, Part I, Sixth Committee, Summary Records of Meetings, 21 September–10 December 1948.

————. Official Records. Fifth Session. *Ad Hoc* Political Committee. 5th Meeting, 5 October 1950.

————. Official Records. Fifth Session. Supplement No. 20. Resolutions Adopted by the General Assembly during the Period 19 September to 15 December 1950.

————. Interim Committee. Report of the Sub-Committee on International Cooperation in the Political Field to the Interim Committee. (United Nations Doc. A/AC.18/114, 5 July 1950).

————. Reports of International Arbitral Awards. 3 vols. 1948-1949. (Prepared by the Registry of the International Court of Justice.)

————. Security Council. Official Records. 5th Year. No. 31. 489th Meeting, 22 August 1950.

————. Department of Public Information. *Yearbook of the United Nations.* (Annual.)

United Nations Conference on International Organization, San Francisco, 1945. *Documents.* 16 vols. London and New York, United Nations Information Organizations, 1945-1946.

United States. Congress. Senate. Committee on Foreign Relations. *Compulsory Jurisdiction, International Court of Jus-*

tice. Hearings before a Sub-committee . . . on Senate Res. 196 . . . 11, 12 and 15 July 1946. Washington, Government Printing Office, 1946.

————. Department of State. Department of State *Bulletin*.

————. Publication 2349. *Charter of the United Nations: Report to the President on the Results of the San Francisco Conference by the Chairman of the United States Delegation, The Secretary of State*. [Washington], 26 June 1945.

————. Publication 2490. *The United Nations Conference on International Organization: Selected Documents*. Washington, Government Printing Office, 1946.

————. Publication 2491. *The International Court of Justice: Selected Documents Relating to the Drafting of the Statute*. Washington, Government Printing Office, 1946.

————. Publication 3540. *Compulsory Jurisdiction of the International Court of Justice*. [Washington, Government Printing Office, 1949].

BOOKS

Brierly, James L. *The Law of Nations*. Fourth Edition. Oxford, The Clarendon Press, 1949.

————. *The Outlook for International Law*. Oxford, The Clarendon Press, 1944.

Carr, Edward Hallett. *The Twenty Years' Crisis 1919-1939*. Second Edition. London, Macmillan Co., 1946.

Collette, Jean. *Les Principes de Droit des Gens dans la Jurisprudence de la Cour Permanente de Justice Internationale*. Paris, Berger-Levrault, 1932.

Derevitzky, Pierre. *Les Principes du Droit International tels qu'ils Se Dégagent de la Jurisprudence de la Cour Permanente de Justice Internationale*. Paris, A. Pedone, 1932.

Dulles, John Foster. *War or Peace*. New York, Macmillan Co., 1950.

Dunn, Frederick Sherwood. *The Protection of Nationals*. Baltimore, The Johns Hopkins Press, 1932.

Fachiri, Alexander P. *The Permanent Court of International Justice: Its Constitution, Procedure and Work*. Second Edition. London, Oxford University Press, 1932.

Feller, A. H. *The Mexican Claims Commissions 1923-1934*. New York, Macmillan Co., 1935.

GOODRICH, LELAND M., AND HAMBRO, EDVARD. *Charter of the United Nations: Commentary and Documents.* Revised Edition. Boston, World Peace Foundation, 1949.

HACKWORTH, GREEN H. *Digest of International Law.* 8 vols. Washington, Government Printing Office, 1940-1944.

HAMBRO, EDVARD. *L'Exécution des Sentences Internationales.* Liège, H. Vaillant-Carmanne, 1936.

HAMMARSKJÖLD, A. *Juridiction Internationale.* Leiden, A. W. Sijthoff, 1938.

HUDSON, MANLEY O. *International Tribunals: Past and Future.* Washington, Carnegie Endowment for International Peace and Brookings Institution, 1944.

————. *The Permanent Court of International Justice 1920-1942.* New York, Macmillan Co., 1943.

HYDE, CHARLES CHENEY. *International Law Chiefly as Interpreted and Applied by the United States.* 3 vols. Second Revised Edition. Boston, Little, Brown and Company, 1945.

JESSUP, PHILIP C. *A Modern Law of Nations.* New York, Macmillan Co., 1948.

JIMÉNEZ DE ARÉCHAGA, EDUARDO. *Voting and the Handling of Disputes in the Security Council.* (United Nations Studies: No. 5.) New York, Carnegie Endowment for International Peace, 1950.

KAUFMANN, HANS. *Die Gutachten des Ständigen Internationalen Gerichtshofes als Mittel zwischenstaatlicher Streitschlichtung.* Basel, Helbing & Lichtenhahn, 1939.

KELSEN, HANS. *General Theory of Law and State.* Cambridge, Harvard University Press, 1945.

————. *Law and Peace in International Relations.* Cambridge, Harvard University Press, 1942.

————. *Peace Through Law.* Chapel Hill, University of North Carolina Press, 1944.

————. *The Law of the United Nations.* New York, Frederick A. Praeger Inc., 1950.

KRYLOV, S. B. *Materialy k Istorii Organizatsii Ob'edinennykh Natsii.* Moscow, Izdatel'stvo Akademii Nauk SSSR, 1949.

LAUTERPACHT, H. *The Development of International Law by the Permanent Court of International Justice.* London, Longmans, Green and Co., 1934.

————. *The Function of Law in the International Community.* Oxford, The Clarendon Press, 1933.

MAGYARY, GÉZA VON. *La Juridiction de la Cour Permanente de Justice Internationale.* Paris, Editions Internationales, 1931.

MILLER, DAVID HUNTER. *The Geneva Protocol.* New York, Macmillan Co., 1925.

MOORE, JOHN BASSETT. *A Digest of International Law.* 8 vols. Washington, Government Printing Office, 1906.

————. *History and Digest of International Arbitrations to Which the United States Has Been a Party.* 6 vols. Washington, Government Printing Office, 1898.

————. *International Law and Some Current Illusions.* New York, Macmillan Co., 1924.

MORGENTHAU, HANS J. *Politics Among Nations.* New York, A. A. Knopf, 1948.

NIEMEYER, GERHART. *Law Without Force.* Princeton, Princeton University Press, 1941.

SCHWARZENBERGER, GEORG. *International Law.* Volume I. *International Law as Applied by International Courts and Tribunals.* Second Edition. London, Stevens & Sons Limited, 1949.

SHOTWELL, JAMES T. AND SALVIN, MARINA. *Lessons on Security and Disarmament from the History of the League of Nations.* New York, Carnegie Endowment for International Peace, 1949.

SMITH, H. A. *The Crisis in the Law of Nations.* London, Stevens & Sons Limited, 1947.

STONE, JULIUS. *The Province and Function of Law.* Sydney, Associated General Publications, 1946.

TARACOUZIO, T. A. *The Soviet Union and International Law.* New York, Macmillan Co., 1935.

VYSHINSKY, A. Y. *Voprosy Mezhdunarodnogo Prava i Mezhdunarodnoi Politiki.* Moscow, Gosudarstvennoe Izdatel'stvo Yuridicheskoi Literatury, 1949.

PAMPHLETS AND ARTICLES

BECKETT, W. E. "Les Questions d'Intérêt Général au Point de Vue Juridique dans la Jurisprudence de la Cour Permanente de Justice Internationale," Académie de Droit International de la Haye, *Recueil des Cours,* 1932-I, p. 131; 1934-IV, p. 189.

BORCHARD, EDWIN M. "The Customs Union Advisory Opinion," *American Journal of International Law,* Vol. 25 (1931), p. 711.

———. "The Impracticability of 'Enforcing' Peace," *Yale Law Journal,* Vol. 55 (1946), p. 966.

BORISOV, S. "Priem Novykh Chlenov v Organizatsiiu Ob'edinennykh Natsii," *Sovetskoe Gosudarstvo i Pravo,* 1948, No. 9, p. 6.

COLLINS, J. FOSTER. "The United Nations and Indonesia," *International Conciliation,* No. 459, March 1950 (New York, Carnegie Endowment for International Peace).

DE VISSCHER, CHARLES. "Les Avis Consultatifs de Cour Permanente de Justice Internationale," Académie de Droit International de la Haye, *Recueil des Cours,* 1929-I, p. 1.

DICKINSON, EDWIN D. "International Law: An Inventory," *California Law Review,* Vol. 33 (1945), p. 506.

DOUGLAS, WILLIAM O. "Stare Decisis," *Columbia Law Review,* Vol. 49 (1949), p. 735.

DUMBAULD, EDWARD. "Relief *Pendente Lite* in the Permanent Court of International Justice," *American Journal of International Law,* Vol. 39 (1945), p. 391.

FREEMAN, HARROP AND PAULLIN, THEODORE. *Coercion of States: In Federal Unions.* Philadelphia, The Pacifist Research Bureau, 1943.

GILMORE, GRANT. "The International Court of Justice," *Yale Law Journal,* Vol. 55 (1946), p. 1049.

GOODRICH, LELAND M. "The Nature of the Advisory Opinions of the Permanent Court of International Justice," *American Journal of International Law,* Vol. 32 (1938), p. 738.

———. "The United Nations and Domestic Jurisdiction," *International Organization,* Vol. III, No. 1, February 1949, p. 14.

GROSS, ERNEST A. "Impact of the United Nations Upon Domestic Jurisdiction," Department of State *Bulletin,* Vol. XVIII (1948), p. 259.

HACKWORTH, GREEN H. "The International Court of Justice and the Codification of International Law," *American Bar Association Journal,* Vol. 32 (1946), p. 81.

HAMBRO, EDVARD. "The International Court of Justice," *The Year Book of World Affairs 1949,* p. 188.

———. "Some Observations on the Compulsory Jurisdiction of the International Court of Justice," *The British Year Book of International Law 1948* (Vol. 25), p. 133.

HUDSON, MANLEY O. Annual articles on the Court in the January issues of *American Journal of International Law;* particularly "The Twenty-Fourth Year of the World Court," *ibid.,* Vol. 40 (1946), p. 1; "The Twenty-Eighth Year of the World Court," *ibid.,* Vol. 44 (1950), p. 1; and "The Twenty-Ninth Year of the World Court," *ibid.,* Vol. 45 (1951), p. 1.

———. "Les Avis Consultatifs de la Cour Permanente de Justice Internationale," Académie de Droit International de la Haye, *Recueil des Cours,* 1925-III, p. 344.

———. "The Effect of Advisory Opinions of the World Court," *American Journal of International Law,* Vol. 42 (1948), p. 630.

HURST, SIR CECIL. "A Plea for the Codification of International Law on New Lines," The Grotius Society, *Transactions for the Year 1946* (Vol. 32), p. 135.

HYDE, CHARLES CHENEY. "Bombs, Super-Bombs, and the Cost of Peace," *Texas Law Review,* Vol. 29 (1950), p. 143.

JENKS, C. WILFRED. "The Status of International Organizations in Relation to the International Court of Justice," Grotius Society, *Transactions for the Year 1946* (Vol. 32), p. 1.

JENNINGS, R. Y. "The Progressive Development of International Law and Its Codification," *The British Year Book of International Law 1947* (Vol. 24), p. 301.

JESSUP, PHILIP C. "The Customs Union Advisory Opinion," *American Journal of International Law,* Vol. 26 (1932), p. 105.

———. "The Growth of the Law," *American Journal of International Law,* Vol. 29 (1935), p. 495.

———. "The International Court of Justice and Legal Matters," *Illinois Law Review,* Vol. 42 (1947), p. 273.

———. "The International Court of Justice of the United Nations," *Foreign Policy Reports,* Vol. 21 (1945), p. 154.

———. "The Reality of International Law," *Foreign Affairs,* Vol. 18 (1940), p. 224.

KELSEN, HANS. "Compulsory Adjudication of International Disputes," *American Journal of International Law,* Vol. 37 (1943), p. 397.

LAUTERPACHT, H. "Restrictive Interpretation and the Principle of Effectiveness in the Interpretation of Treaties," *The British Year Book of International Law 1949* (Vol. 26), p. 48.

LEONARD, L. LARRY. "The United Nations and Palestine," *International Conciliation,* No. 454, October 1949 (New York, Carnegie Endowment for International Peace).

LIANG, YUEN-LI. "Notes on Legal Questions Concerning the United Nations," *American Journal of International Law,* Vol. 42 (1948), p. 435.

MCDOUGAL, MYRES S. "The Role of Law in World Politics," *Mississippi Law Journal,* Vol. XX, (1949), p. 253.

MOORE, JOHN BASSETT. "The Question of Advisory Opinions," *The Collected Works of John Bassett Moore,* New Haven, Yale University Press, 1944, Vol. V, p. 329.

NEGULESCU, DÉMÈTRE. "L'Evolution de la Procédure des Avis Consultatifs de la Cour Permanente de Justice Internationale," Académie de Droit International de la Haye, *Recueil des Cours,* 1936-III, p. 1.

PREUSS, LAWRENCE. "The International Court of Justice and the Problem of Compulsory Jurisdiction," Department of State *Bulletin,* Vol. XIII (1945), p. 471.

————. "The International Court of Justice, the Senate, and Matters of Domestic Jurisdiction," *American Journal of International Law,* Vol. 40 (1946), p. 720.

ROSENBERG, JAMES N. "*Brutum Fulmen:* A Precedent for a World Court," *Columbia Law Review,* Vol. 25 (1925), p. 783.

RUBIN, SEYMOUR J. "The Judicial Review Problem in the International Trade Organization," *Harvard Law Review,* Vol. 63 (1949), p. 78.

SCHWARZENBERGER, GEORG. "International Law and Society," *The Year Book of World Affairs 1947,* p. 159.

————. "The Rule of Law and the Disintegration of the International Society," *American Journal of International Law,* Vol. 33 (1939), p. 56.

SLOAN, F. BLAINE. "Advisory Jurisdiction of the International Court of Justice," *California Law Review,* Vol. 38 (1950), p. 830.

————. "Comparative International and Municipal Law Sanctions," *Nebraska Law Review,* Vol. 27 (1947), p. 1.

———. "Enforcement of Arbitral Awards in International Agencies," *The Arbitration Journal,* New Series, Vol. III (1948), p. 134.

SOHN, LOUIS B. "Exclusion of Political Disputes from Judicial Settlement," *American Journal of International Law,* Vol. 38 (1944), p. 694.

VULCAN, CONSTANTIN. "L'Exécution des Décisions de la Cour Internationale de Justice d'après la Charte des Nations Unies," *Revue Générale de Droit International Public,* Vol. 51 (1947), p. 187.

VYSHINSKY, A. Y. "Mezhdunarodnoe Pravo i Mezhdunarodnaia Organizatsiia," *Sovetskoe Gosudarstvo i Pravo,* 1948, No. 1, p. 1.

WARREN, CHARLES. "The Supreme Court and Disputes Between States," *International Conciliation,* No. 366, January 1941, p. 20 (New York, Carnegie Endowment for International Peace).

WILCOX, FRANCIS O. "The United States Accepts Compulsory Jurisdiction," *American Journal of International Law,* Vol. 40 (1946), p. 699.

WRIGHT, QUINCY. "The International Court of Justice and the Interpretation of Multilateral Treaties," *American Journal of International Law,* Vol. 41 (1947), p. 445.